Bless Your Heart

Series II

Dear Reader,

What a joy it has been to prepare a new **Bless Your Heart** perpetual calendar for you. Those of us who have the privilege of doing the research receive a double blessing!

Heartland Samplers' staff prays for you weekly. Our purpose is to encourage people and to make an eternal difference in their lives by providing superior products which are scripturally sound and of excellent value.

We appreciate the encouragement that we receive from you and pray that you will be blessed and encouraged as you use this new calendar.

Heartland Samplers, Inc.

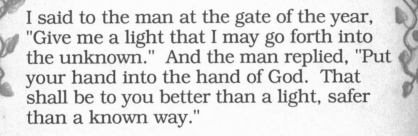

I said to the man at the gate of the year, "Give me a light that I may go forth into the unknown." And the man replied, "Put your hand into the hand of God. That shall be to you better than a light, safer than a known way."

(A New Year's message from Britain's King George to his embattled people at the beginning of WWII.)

JANUARY 1

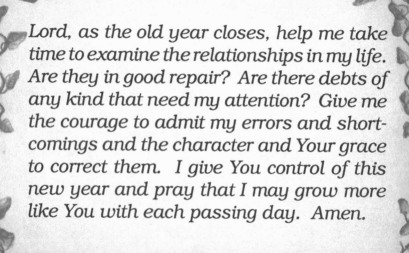

Lord, as the old year closes, help me take time to examine the relationships in my life. Are they in good repair? Are there debts of any kind that need my attention? Give me the courage to admit my errors and short-comings and the character and Your grace to correct them. I give You control of this new year and pray that I may grow more like You with each passing day. Amen.

DECEMBER 31

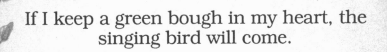

If I keep a green bough in my heart, the singing bird will come.

...Always be prepared to give an answer to everyone who asks you to give the reason for the hope that you have.

I Peter 3:15 NIV

JANUARY 2

No one knows what this next year will bring, but one thing is sure.
He will be with us and He is enough for every difficulty that may arise.

Amy Carmichael

Do not be afraid or terrified...for the Lord your God goes with you; he will never leave you or forsake you.

Deut. 31:6 NIV

DECEMBER 30

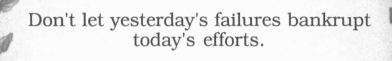

Don't let yesterday's failures bankrupt today's efforts.

Commit to the Lord whatever you do, and your plans will succeed. The Lord works out everything for His own ends.

Prov. 16:3 & 4 NIV

JANUARY 3

For you have a new life.
It was not passed on to you from your
parents, for the life they gave you will
fade away.
This new one will last forever, for it comes
from Christ, God's ever-living message
to men.

I Pet. 1:23 TLB

*I do desire to have a new life. You know I
have sinned Father. I confess my sins
and ask Your forgiveness. I pray that
You will take my life and make me a new
creation. Amen.*

DECEMBER 29

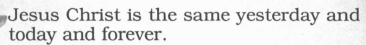

Jesus Christ is the same yesterday and today and forever.

Heb. 13:8 NIV

Dear Lord, my world has turned upside down; everything is so uncertain and frightening. I am thankful for your unchanging love and constant support. Amen.

JANUARY 4

Dear Friends,
you who are letting miserable misunderstandings run on from year to year, meaning to clear them up some day;...You who are passing man sullenly upon the street, not speaking out of some silly spite, and yet knowing that it would fill you with remorse if you heard that one of these men were dead tomorrow morning; you who are...letting your friend's heart ache for a word of appreciation or sympathy, which you mean to give him some day– if you could know...that "the time is short", how it would break the spell! How you would go instantly and do the thing which you might never have another chance to do.

The Time is Short
Phillip Brooks

DECEMBER 28

If you live for the next world, you get this one in the deal; but if you live only for this world, you lose them both.

C.S. Lewis

If anyone would come after me, he must deny himself and take up his cross daily and follow me...What good is it for a man to gain the whole world, and yet lose or forfeit his very self?

Luke 9:23 & 25 NIV

JANUARY 5

Watch for good times to retreat into yourself. Frequently meditate on how good God is to you.

T. a Kempis

The hours fly by and I am always in a rush...so many duties and relationships to tend to, Lord. Help me find the time to meditate on the most important relationship of all—my relationship with You. Amen.

DECEMBER 27

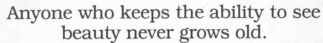

Anyone who keeps the ability to see beauty never grows old.

Franz Kafka

One thing I ask of the Lord, this is what I seek: that I may dwell in the house of the Lord all the days of my life, to gaze upon the beauty of the Lord and to seek Him in His temple.

Psalm 27:4 NIV

JANUARY 6

Sometimes, Father, frigid winter blankets my Spirit. Gray days become a harsh and heavy burden.

And then I remember how you promised Noah winter and summer, seedtime and harvest, day and night, cold and heat as long as the earth shall live.

Help me to understand; the barren and difficult times are not a curse, but part of a blessing—Your wonderful, everchanging gift: **life**.

Guideposts

DECEMBER 26

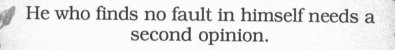

He who finds no fault in himself needs a
second opinion.

He who listens to a life-giving rebuke will
be at home among the wise.

Proverbs 15:30 NIV

JANUARY 7

Behold, what manner of love
the Father hath given unto us...
I John 3:1

DECEMBER   25

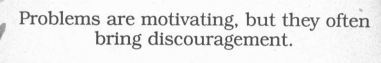

Problems are motivating, but they often
bring discouragement.

*Lord, when I am discouraged and can see
no way out, I need You by my side. Please
meet me right where I am and walk with
me through the day. Thank You. Amen.*

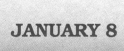

JANUARY 8

If our need had been **information**,
  God would have sent us an **educator**.
If our need had been **technology**,
  God would have sent us a **scientist**.
If our need had been **money,**
  God would have sent us an **economist**.
If our need had been **pleasure**,
  God would have sent us an **entertainer**.
But our greatest need was **forgiveness**,
  so God sent us a **Savior.**

But God demonstrates his own love for us in this: While we were still sinners, Christ died for us. Rom. 5:8 NIV

DECEMBER 24

Worry is interest paid on trouble before it comes due.

William Ralph Inge

...do not worry about your life, what you will eat or drink; or about your body, what you will wear. Who of you by worrying can add a single hour to his life?

Matt. 6:25 & 27 NIV

JANUARY 9

The most important part about Christmas
is the first six letters.

...I bring you good news of great joy that will
be for all the people.

...a Savior has been born to you; he is Christ
the Lord.

Luke 2:10 & 11 NIV

DECEMBER 23

Real difficulties can be overcome; it is only
the imaginary ones that are
unconquerable.

Theodore Vail

Do not be anxious about anything, but in
everything, by prayer and petition, with
thanksgiving, present your requests to
God. And the peace of God, which
transcends all understanding, will guard
your hearts and your minds in Christ
Jesus.

Phil. 4: 6 & 7 NIV

JANUARY 10

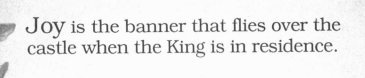

Joy is the banner that flies over the castle when the King is in residence.

May he give you the desire of your heart and make all your plans succeed. We will shout for joy when you are victorious and will lift up our banners in the name of our God. May the Lord grant all your requests.

Ps. 20: 4 & 5 NIV

DECEMBER 22

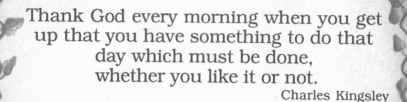

Thank God every morning when you get
up that you have something to do that
day which must be done,
whether you like it or not.

Charles Kingsley

*Oh, Lord, I thank You for the purpose and
hope Your love provides. Help me to
appreciate the tasks You have set before
me. Amen.*

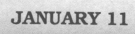

JANUARY 11

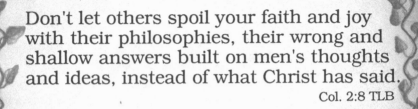

Don't let others spoil your faith and joy with their philosophies, their wrong and shallow answers built on men's thoughts and ideas, instead of what Christ has said.

Col. 2:8 TLB

Lord, how can it be that in my search, I so quickly pass You by.? In this season of giving, help me remember that You are the gift; already given for me if I am willing to receive You. Amen.

DECEMBER 21

Where there is hatred——let me sow love.
Where there is injury——pardon.
Where there is doubt——faith.
Where there is darkness—light.
Where there is despair——hope.
Where there is sadness—joy.

St. Francis of Assisi

Commit to the Lord whatever you do, and your plans will succeed.

Prov.16:3 NIV

JANUARY 12

When Light comes, the shadow can no longer exist.

In him was life, and that life was the light of man. The light shines in the darkness, but the darkness has not understood it.

John 1: 4 & 5 NIV

DECEMBER 20

Anxious hearts are very heavy but a word of encouragement does wonders!

Prov. 12:25 TLB

Father, help me remember that my words have power—power to encourage and power to discourage. Help me speak kind words and bring encouragement. Amen.

JANUARY 13

Beware of the barreness of a busy life.
Socrates

Dear Father, help me be diligent in maintaining a meaningful inner life, remembering that time spent with You gives my life meaning and fruitfulness. Amen.

DECEMBER 19

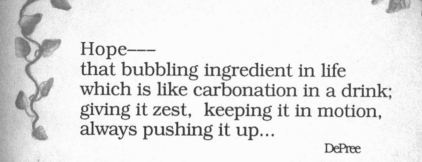

Hope———
that bubbling ingredient in life
which is like carbonation in a drink;
giving it zest, keeping it in motion,
always pushing it up...

DePree

Lord, you alone are my hope...

Ps. 71:5 TLB

JANUARY 14

I have been driven many times to my knees by the overwhelming conviction that I had nowhere else to go.

Abraham Lincoln

...when you pray, go into your room and shut the door and pray to your Father who is in secret...

Matt. 6:6 RSV

DECEMBER 18

What does the Lord require of you? To act justly and to love mercy and to walk humbly with your God.

Micah 6:8 NIV

O Lord, for me to walk humbly with You, You need to be in control of my life. Please help me as I begin this new year to allow You to be in control. My heart's desire is to please You. Amen.

JANUARY 15

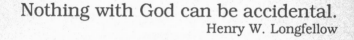

Nothing with God can be accidental.
Henry W. Longfellow

"...I know the plans I have for you", declares the Lord, "plans to prosper you and not to harm you, plans to give you hope and a future."

Jer. 29:11 NIV

DECEMBER 17

If a man is called to be a streetsweeper, he should sweep streets even as Michelangelo painted, or Beethoven composed music, or Shakespeare wrote poetry. He should sweep streets so well that all the hosts of heaven and earth will pause to say, here lived a great streetsweeper who did his job well.

Martin Luther King, Jr.

Whatever your hand finds to do, do it with all your might...

Ecc. 9:10 NIV

JANUARY 16

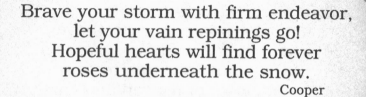

Brave your storm with firm endeavor,
let your vain repinings go!
Hopeful hearts will find forever
roses underneath the snow.

Cooper

Hope does not disappoint us, because God
has poured out his love into our hearts by
the Holy Spirit, whom he has given us.

Rom. 5:5 NIV

DECEMBER 16

The point of having an open mind, like having an open mouth, is to close it on something solid.

G.K. Chesterton

Do not let this Book of the Law depart from your mouth; meditate on it day and night, so that you may be careful to do everything written in it.

Josh. 1:8 NIV

JANUARY 17

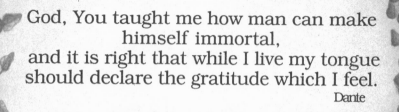

God, You taught me how man can make
himself immortal,
and it is right that while I live my tongue
should declare the gratitude which I feel.

Dante

Yet to all who received him, to those who
believed in his name, he gave the right to
become children of God.

John 1:12 NIV

DECEMBER 15

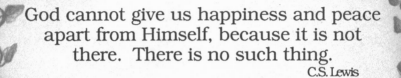

God cannot give us happiness and peace apart from Himself, because it is not there. There is no such thing.

C.S. Lewis

Peace I leave with you; my peace I give you. I do not give to you as the world gives. Do not let your hearts be troubled and do not be afraid.

John 14:27 NIV

JANUARY 18

The world crowns success, but God crowns faithfulness.

...never tire of doing what is right.

II Thess. 3:13 NIV

A faithful man will be richly blessed...

Prov. 28:20 NIV

DECEMBER 14

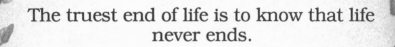

The truest end of life is to know that life
never ends.

Now this is eternal life: that they may
know you, the only true God, and Jesus
Christ, whom you have sent.

John 17:3 NIV

JANUARY 19

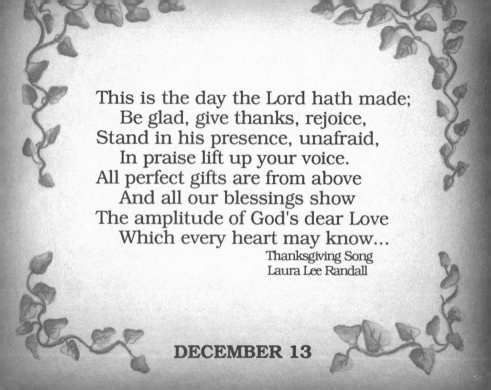

This is the day the Lord hath made;
  Be glad, give thanks, rejoice,
Stand in his presence, unafraid,
  In praise lift up your voice.
All perfect gifts are from above
  And all our blessings show
The amplitude of God's dear Love
  Which every heart may know...

Thanksgiving Song
Laura Lee Randall

DECEMBER 13

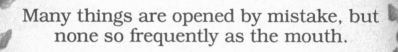

Many things are opened by mistake, but none so frequently as the mouth.

Time and words cannot be recalled.

Lord, help me to remember the things I ought not to forget, and to forget the things I ought not to remember. Amen.

JANUARY 20

What are you saving in your memory bin as food for the restless soul when the winter of life comes?

Lord, what would You have me store in my memory? Help me remember the times I have seen Your hand in my life and to be thankful for the many blessings You have provided. Amen.

DECEMBER 12

It is a great error to take oneself for more than one is, or for less than one is worth.

Goethe

So God created man in his own image, in the image of God he created him; male and female he created them...God saw all that he had made, and it was very good...

Gen. 1:27-31 NIV

JANUARY 21

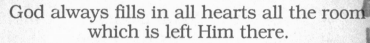

God always fills in all hearts all the room
which is left Him there.

F.W. Faber

The Lord Your God is with you, he is
mighty to save. He will take great delight in
you, he will quiet you with his love, he will
rejoice over you with singing.

Zeph. 3:17 NIV

DECEMBER 11

And He will raise you up on eagle's wings
bear you on the breath of dawn,
make you to shine like the sun,
and hold you in the palm of His hand.

African Song

...but those who hope in the Lord will renew their strength. They will soar on wings like eagles; they will run and not grow weary, they will walk and not be faint.

Is. 40:31 NIV

JANUARY 22

Life holds no sweeter thing than this:
To teach a little child the tale most loved
   on earth
And watch the wonder deepen in his eyes
The while you tell him of the Christ
   Child's birth;
The while you tell of shepherds and a
      song,
Of gentle drowsy beasts and fragrant hay
On which that starlit night in Bethlehem
God's tiny Son and His young mother
lay...

Adelaide Love

DECEMBER 10

We always have time for
the things we put first.

But seek first his kingdom and his
righteousness, and all these things will be
given to you as well.

Matt. 6:33 NIV

JANUARY 23

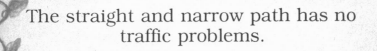

The straight and narrow path has no traffic problems.

Enter through the narrow gate. For wide is the gate and broad is the road that leads to destruction... But small is the gate and narrow the road that leads to life...

Matt. 7:13 & 14 NIV

DECEMBER 9

All Truth is God's Truth.

For the law was given through Moses; grace and truth came through Jesus Christ.

John 1:17 NIV

Open my eyes to the Truth, Lord, and help me to be strengthened by it today that I might serve You. Amen.

JANUARY 24

A good conscience is a continual Christmas.

Benjamin Franklin

...let us draw near to God with a sincere heart in full assurance of faith, having our hearts sprinkled to cleanse us from a guilty conscience.

Heb. 10:22 NIV

DECEMBER 8

May you never miss a rainbow or sunset because you are looking down.

I will lift up mine eyes unto the hills from whence cometh my help. My help cometh from the Lord...

Ps. 121:1 & 2 KJV

JANUARY 25

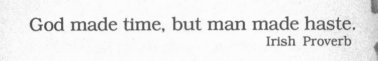

God made time, but man made haste.
Irish Proverb

The plans of the diligent lead to profit as surely as haste leads to poverty.
Prov. 21:5 NIV

DECEMBER 7

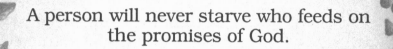

A person will never starve who feeds on the promises of God.

Not one word has failed of all the good promises he gave through his servant Moses.

I Kings 8:56 NIV

JANUARY 26

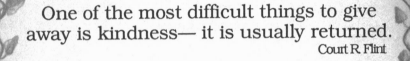

One of the most difficult things to give away is kindness— it is usually returned.

Court R. Flint

...but with everlasting kindness I will have compassion on you says the Lord your Redeemer.

Is. 54:8 NIV

DECEMBER 6

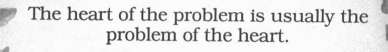

The heart of the problem is usually the problem of the heart.

Love the Lord your God with all your heart and with all your soul and with all your mind and with all your strength.

Mark 12:30 NIV

JANUARY 27

Great works are performed not by strength, but by perseverance.

Samuel Johnson

By perseverance the snail reached the ark.

C.H. Spurgeon

Perseverance must finish its work so that you may be mature and complete, not lacking anything.

James 1:4 NIV

DECEMBER 5

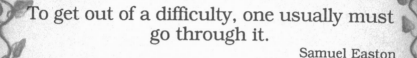

To get out of a difficulty, one usually must go through it.

Samuel Easton

...along unfamiliar paths I will guide them; I will turn the darkness into light before them and make the rough places smooth.

Is. 42:16 NIV

JANUARY 28

Oh would some power the gift give us,
to see ourselves as others see us.

Robert Burns

For the Lord sees not as man sees, man
looks on the outward appearance, but
the Lord looks on the heart.

I Sam. 16:7 RSV

DECEMBER 4

Praise is more spontaneous when things go right; but it is more precious when things go wrong.

It is good to praise the Lord and make music to your name, O Most High, to proclaim your love in the morning and your faithfulness at night...

Ps. 92:1 & 2 NIV

JANUARY 29

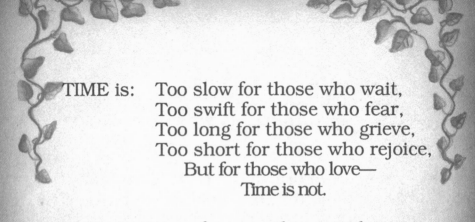

TIME is: Too slow for those who wait,
Too swift for those who fear,
Too long for those who grieve,
Too short for those who rejoice,
But for those who love—
Time is not.

There is a time for everything, and a
season for every activity under heaven.

Ecc. 3:1 NIV

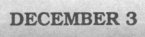

DECEMBER 3

Those who live in the Lord never see each other for the last time.

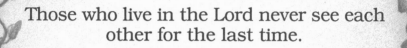

..."Death has been swallowed up in victory. Where, O death, is your victory? Where, O death, is your sting?"

I Cor. 15:54 & 55 NIV

JANUARY 30

Youth is not a time of life—— it is a state of mind. Nobody grows old by merely living a number of years; people grow old only by deserting their ideals. Years wrinkle the skin, but to give up enthusiasm wrinkles the soul.

May the God of hope fill you with all joy and peace as you trust in him, so that you may overflow with hope by the power of the Holy Spirit.

Romans 15:13 NIV

DECEMBER 2

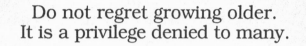

Do not regret growing older.
It is a privilege denied to many.

Teach us to number our days aright, that
we may gain a heart of wisdom.

Ps. 90:12 NIV

JANUARY 31

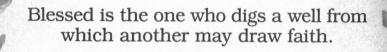

Blessed is the one who digs a well from which another may draw faith.

Choose my instruction instead of silver, knowledge rather than choice gold, for wisdom is more precious than rubies, and nothing you desire can compare with her.

Prov. 8:10 & 11 NIV

DECEMBER 1

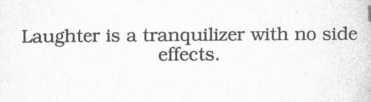

Laughter is a tranquilizer with no side
effects.

A cheerful look brings joy to the heart,
and good news gives health to the bones.

Prov. 15:30 NIV

FEBRUARY 1

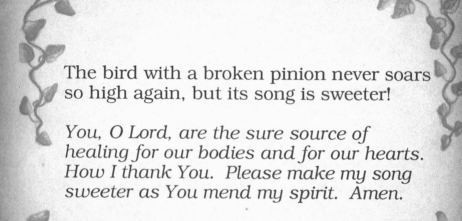

The bird with a broken pinion never soars so high again, but its song is sweeter!

You, O Lord, are the sure source of healing for our bodies and for our hearts. How I thank You. Please make my song sweeter as You mend my spirit. Amen.

NOVEMBER 30

Love the Lord your God with all your heart and with all your soul and with all your strength. These commandments that I give you today are to be upon your hearts. Impress them on your children. Talk about them when you sit at home and when you walk along the road, when you lie down and when you get up. Write them on the doorframes of your houses and on your gates.

Deut. 6:4-9 NIV

But if you seek the Lord your God, you will find him if you look for him with all your heart and with all your soul.

Deut. 4:29 NIV

FEBRUARY 2

There is no right way to do the wrong thing.

Character is a victory, not a gift.

Lord, You know that I often turn circumstances 'round and 'round trying to make the wrong thing seem right. Thank You for the victories won when I bring these circumstances to You and follow Your direction. Help me to walk in a way pleasing to You. Amen.

NOVEMBER 29

His daily prayer, far better understood in acts than in words, was simply doing good.

John Greenleaf Whittier

Jesus replied, "...Love your neighbor as yourself."

Matt. 22:37-39 NIV

"I tell you the truth, whatever you did for one of the least of these brothers of mine you did for me."

Matt. 25:40 NIV

FEBRUARY 3

There are three things difficult:
  -to keep a secret,
  -to suffer an injury,
  -to use leisure.

Voltaire

Lord, it is especially hard for me to take leisure time. I need more balance in my life. "Be imitators of God", You commanded; help me learn to rest as You did. Please give me the desire to imitate You in this and every area of my life. Amen.

NOVEMBER 28

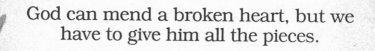

God can mend a broken heart, but we
have to give him all the pieces.

The Lord is close to the brokenhearted
and saves those who are crushed in spirit.

Ps. 34:18 NIV

FEBRUARY 4

Better the storm with Christ than smooth waters without Him.

...When you pass through the waters, I will be with you... Is. 43:2 NIV

Thank You for this wonderful reassurance Father. I need You to go with me; I cannot continue on alone. I place my storm and my life in Your hands. Amen.

NOVEMBER 27

I may be old but I haven't stopped growing!

O.W. Holmes, Jr.

Oh, Lord, may this be true of me. As I grow older, may I also grow wiser in Your knowledge and wisdom, and more loving in Your Spirit. Amen.

FEBRUARY 5

Life must be measured by thought and action, not by time.   Lubbock

How hard this is to do, Lord. Everything seems to be measured by time, yet I know there are those whose lives are in need of Your love. Help me move outside of time and carry Your hope to those You put into my path daily. Amen.

NOVEMBER 26

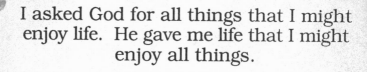

I asked God for all things that I might enjoy life. He gave me life that I might enjoy all things.

Oh, Lord, how like You to give me what I need instead of what I ask for. Thank You for always providing the best for me and helping me see that all things come to me through Your hand. Amen.

FEBRUARY 6

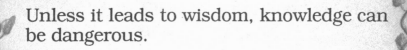

Unless it leads to wisdom, knowledge can be dangerous.

...I consider everything a loss compared to the surpassing greatness of knowing Christ Jesus my Lord...   Phil. 3:8 NIV

NOVEMBER 25

As for old age, embrace it and love it.
It abounds with pleasure, if you know
how to use it.
The gradually declining years are
amongst the sweetest...and I maintain,
that even where they have reached the
extreme limit, they have their pleasure
still.
Seneca

...Keep my commands in your heart, for
they will prolong your life many years
and bring you prosperity. Prov 32:1 & 2 NIV

FEBRUARY 7

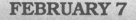

A grudge is one thing that does not get better when it is nursed.

Do not seek revenge or bear a grudge against one of your people, but love your neighbor as yourself.   Lev. 19:18 NIV

Lord, help me be kind and forgiving, for, You know that I need forgiveness. Help me be willing to forgive just as I experience Your forgiveness. Amen.

NOVEMBER 24

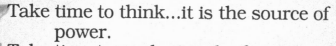

Take time to think...it is the source of
    power.
Take time to read...it is the fountain of
    wisdom.
Take time to pray...it is the greatest power
    on earth.

There is a time for everything, and a
season for every activity under heaven...
                                    Ecc. 3:1 NIV

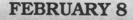

FEBRUARY 8

There has never been a great or beautiful character which has not become so by filling well, the ordinary and smaller offices appointed by God.   Bushnell

Commit your way to the Lord; trust in him and he will do this: He will make your righteousness shine like the dawn, the justice of your cause like the noonday sun.   Ps. 37:5 & 6 NIV

NOVEMBER 23

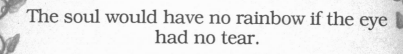

The soul would have no rainbow if the eye had no tear.

Father, how often I rush to wipe away the tear without taking time to see the rainbow that You have provided. Please help me take time to see Your touch in my tears. Amen.

FEBRUARY 9

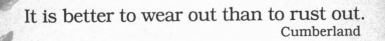

It is better to wear out than to rust out.
Cumberland

...but those who hope in the Lord will renew their strength. They will soar on wings like eagles; they will run and not grow weary, they will walk and not be faint.
Is. 40:31 NIV

NOVEMBER 22

He has the right to criticize who has the heart to help.

Abraham Lincoln

Father, so often I have said one thing with my lips and held another thought in my heart. Please help me live consistently with Your love. Amen.

FEBRUARY 10

To see God in everything makes life the greatest adventure there is.

How true this is, Father! Help me look beyond the fear of the unknown to see You in everything. Renew in me the sense of adventure that comes from walking with and trusting in You. Amen.

NOVEMBER 21

Every morning lean thine arms awhile
upon the window sill of Heaven and gaze
upon the Lord.

Then, with that vision in thy heart
turn strong to meet the day.

*Oh, Lord, Your power and majesty paint
the universe in shimmering glory. Help
me to see the good of Your creation in
everyone. Amen.*

FEBRUARY 11

The most flammable type of wood is a chip on the shoulder.

Get rid of all bitterness, rage and anger...forgiving each other, just as in Christ, God forgave you.

Eph. 4:31 & 32 NIV

NOVEMBER 20

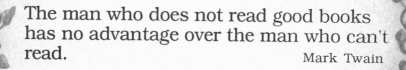

The man who does not read good books has no advantage over the man who can't read.

Mark Twain

I have hidden your Word in my heart that I might not sin against you.   Ps. 119:11 NIV

FEBRUARY 12

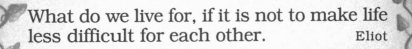

What do we live for, if it is not to make life less difficult for each other.   Eliot

" 'Love the Lord your God with all your heart and with all your soul and with all your mind.' This is the first and greatest commandment. And the second is like it: 'Love your neighbor as yourself...'"

Matt. 22:37-39 NIV

NOVEMBER 19

If you will call your troubles experiences, and remember that every experience develops some latent force within you, you will grow vigorous and happy, however adverse your circumstances may seem to be.

John R. Miller

I have learned the secret of being content in any and every situation, whether well fed or hungry, whether living in plenty or in want. I can do everything through him who gives me strength.

Phil. 4:12 &13 NIV

FEBRUARY 13

So friend,
   when your nights are filled with loneliness and your days are dark with discouragement— when you can't seem to read or pray or to do anything else— just sit still and let God love you.

Father, please encircle my friend with Your arms of love —I pray that Your presence will fill the emptiness of this moment. Amen.

NOVEMBER 18

The steadfast love of the Lord never ceases, his mercies never come to an end; they are new every morning; great is thy faithfulness. Lam. 3:22 & 23 RSV

Thank You, Father, for Your example of love. Your steadfastness, mercy, and faithfulness is such a model for me. Give me Your strength to love others as You have loved me. Amen.

FEBRUARY 14

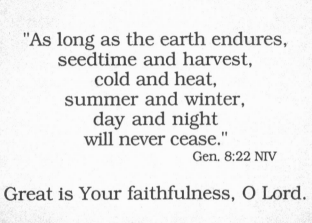

"As long as the earth endures,
seedtime and harvest,
cold and heat,
summer and winter,
day and night
will never cease."
Gen. 8:22 NIV

Great is Your faithfulness, O Lord.

NOVEMBER 17

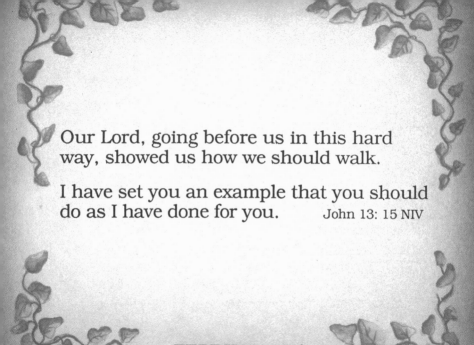

Our Lord, going before us in this hard way, showed us how we should walk.

I have set you an example that you should do as I have done for you.   John 13: 15 NIV

FEBRUARY 15

The weakest among us has a gift, however seemingly trivial, which is peculiar to him, and which worthily used, will be a gift also to his race.

Ruskin

Lord, help me never to scoff at another's weakness or to try to cover my own. Instead, help me encourage others and hold my weaknesses up to You for healing. Amen.

NOVEMBER 16

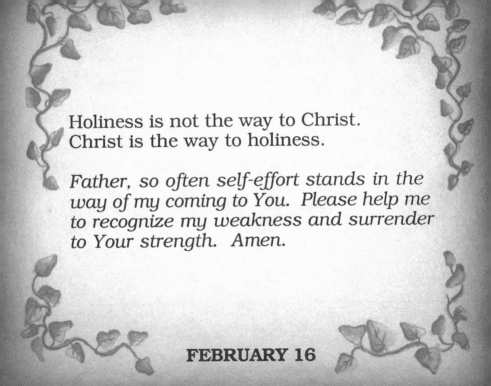

Holiness is not the way to Christ.
Christ is the way to holiness.

*Father, so often self-effort stands in the
way of my coming to You. Please help me
to recognize my weakness and surrender
to Your strength. Amen.*

FEBRUARY 16

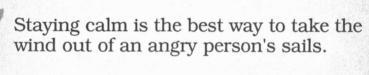

Staying calm is the best way to take the wind out of an angry person's sails.

He who is slow to anger is better than the mighty.

Prov. 16:32 RSV

NOVEMBER 15

There is nothing——nothing——nothing we can do to make God love us more.

Tom Correll

O Lord, please keep me from expecting so much from others and so little from You. Please help me remember that You have given Your life to show me Your love and that is all I need -- nothing more. Amen.

FEBRUARY 17

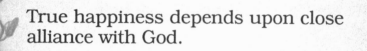

True happiness depends upon close alliance with God.

He will cover you with his feathers, and under his wings you will find refuge; his faithfulness will be your shield...

Ps. 91:4 NIV

NOVEMBER 14

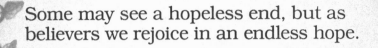

Some may see a hopeless end, but as believers we rejoice in an endless hope.

Always be prepared to give an answer to everyone who asks you to give the reason for the hope that you have. For Christ died for sins once for all, the righteous for the unrighteous to bring you to God...

I Pet. 3:15 & 18 NIV

FEBRUARY 18

There are two freedoms— the false, where a man is free to do what he likes; and the true, where a man is free to do what he ought.

Kingsley

Show me your ways, O Lord, teach me your paths; guide me in your truth...my hope is in you all day long.

Ps. 25:4 & 5 NIV

NOVEMBER 13

We can do no great things, only small things with great love.

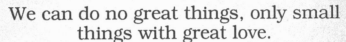

Mother Teresa

Make me aware, Lord, that today never returns. Give me Your great love to do small things this day that count for You. Amen.

FEBRUARY 19

Sympathy gives us the material for wisdom.

The heart of the wise is in the house of the mourning...

Prov. 7:4 NIV

Walk with me as I go to my friend in sorrow. I never know what to say — words never seem sufficient. Give me the strength to go and just be silent, bringing Your love just by being there. Amen.

NOVEMBER 12

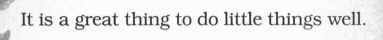

It is a great thing to do little things well.

God comforts us to make us comforters not comfortable.

To ease another's heartache is to forget one's own.

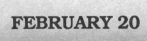

FEBRUARY 20

Whatever one possesses becomes of double value when we have the opportunity of sharing it with others.

Bouilly

But when you give to the needy, do not let your left hand know what your right hand is doing so that your giving may be in secret.

Matt. 6:3 & 4 NIV

NOVEMBER 11

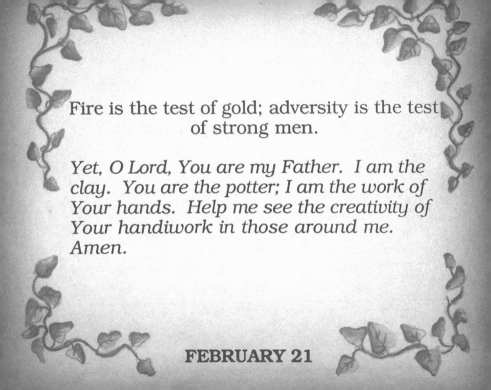

Fire is the test of gold; adversity is the test
of strong men.

*Yet, O Lord, You are my Father. I am the
clay. You are the potter; I am the work of
Your hands. Help me see the creativity of
Your handiwork in those around me.
Amen.*

FEBRUARY 21

How beautiful a day can be when kindness
touches it. Elliston

Love is patient, love is kind. It does not
envy, it does not boast, it is not proud.
Love never fails.. I Cor. 13:4 & 8 NIV

NOVEMBER 10

Your sin will follow you like a shadow.
Verse

Lord, how thankful I am that You have made a provision for me to be rid of the shadow of sin. Help me to daily confess my sin and receive Your forgiveness. Thank You. Amen.

I, even I, am he who blots out your transgressions, for my own sake, and remembers your sins no more.

Is. 43:25 NIV

FEBRUARY 22

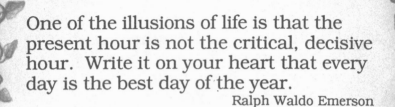

One of the illusions of life is that the present hour is not the critical, decisive hour. Write it on your heart that every day is the best day of the year.

Ralph Waldo Emerson

Teach us to number our days aright, that we may gain a heart of wisdom.

Ps. 90:12 NIV

NOVEMBER 9

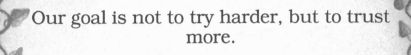

Our goal is not to try harder, but to trust more.

For it is by grace you have been saved, through faith—— and this not from yourselves, it is the gift of God——not by works, so that no one can boast. For we are God's workmanship... Eph.2:8-10 NIV

FEBRUARY 23

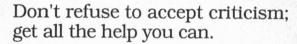

Don't refuse to accept criticism;
get all the help you can.

Prov. 23:12 TLB

*Lord, You know how hard it is for me to
accept criticism. Please help me be open
and receptive to You speaking to me
through others. Amen.*

NOVEMBER 8

I am not what I ought to be.
I am not what I wish to be.
I am not even what I hope to be.

But by God's grace and Christ's love
I am not what I was.

This is what the Lord says to you:
"Do not be afraid or discouraged... For the
battle is not yours but God's."

II Chron. 20:15 NIV

FEBRUARY 24

Why should we be in such desperate haste to succeed, and in such desperate enterprises? If a man does not keep pace with his companions, perhaps it's because he hears a different drummer. Let him step to the music which he hears, however measured or far away.

Henry D. Thoreau

...He has also set eternity in the hearts of men...that everyone may eat and drink, and find satisfaction in all his toil— this is the gift of God.

Ecc. 3:11 & 13 NIV

NOVEMBER 7

Contentment is not the fulfillment of what you want, but the realization of how much you already have.

My God will meet all your needs according to His glorious riches in Christ Jesus.

Phil. 4:19 NIV

It is not how much we have but how much we enjoy, that makes happiness.

C. H. Spurgeon

FEBRUARY 25

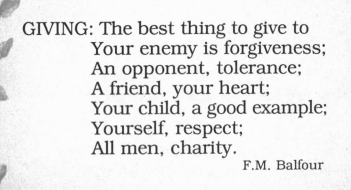

GIVING: The best thing to give to
　　　　Your enemy is forgiveness;
　　　　An opponent, tolerance;
　　　　A friend, your heart;
　　　　Your child, a good example;
　　　　Yourself, respect;
　　　　All men, charity.

F.M. Balfour

NOVEMBER 6

Nothing is worth more than today.

Goethe

Lord, help me have a generous heart. I go through life so quickly that I often forget to take the time to notice the needs of those around me. Give me the grace to respond with Your love to those You put in my path. Amen.

This is the day that the Lord has made. Let us rejoice and be glad in it.

Ps 118:24 NIV

FEBRUARY 26

...for being saved is a gift; if a person could earn it by being good, then it wouldn't be free—but it is!...God declares sinners to be good in his sight if they have faith in Christ.

Rom. 4:4 & 5 TLB

Jesus, thankYou for the gift of Your life on the cross as a sacrifice for my wrongdoings. Please accept my repentance and make me Yours. Amen.

NOVEMBER 5

No one can go back and make a brand
new start, my Friend,

But anyone can start from here and
make a brand new end.

He will be the sure foundation for your
times, a rich store of salvation and
wisdom and knowledge; the fear of the
Lord is the key to this treasure.

Is. 33:6 NIV

FEBRUARY 27

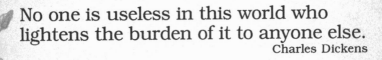

No one is useless in this world who
lightens the burden of it to anyone else.
Charles Dickens

Carry each other's burdens, and in this
way you will fulfill the law of Christ.
Gal 6:2 NIV

NOVEMBER 4

You cannot repent too soon, for you know not how soon it may be too late.

Seek the Lord while he may be found; call on him while he is near. Is. 55:6 NIV

FEBRUARY 28

(No action) can touch us except with (the Father's) knowledge and by His permission... by the time it reaches us it has become God's will for us, and must be accepted as directly from His hands.

Hannah Whitehall Smith

"For I know the plans I have for you," declares the Lord, "plans to prosper you and not to harm you, plans to give you hope and a future."

Jer.29:11NIV

NOVEMBER 3

Restoration always seems to bring joy.

...the ransomed of the Lord will return. They will enter Zion with singing; everlasting joy will crown their heads. Gladness and joy will overtake them, and sorrow and sighing will flee away.

Isaiah 35: 10 NIV

FEBRUARY 29

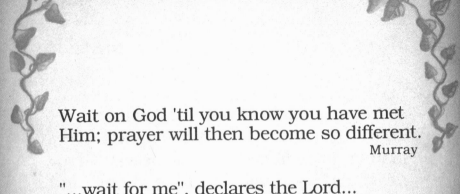

Wait on God 'til you know you have met Him; prayer will then become so different.
Murray

"...wait for me", declares the Lord...
Zeph. 3:8 NIV

NOVEMBER 2

Now and then it is good to pause in our pursuit of happiness and just be happy.

Dear Father, I have so much for which to be thankful—so many reasons to be happy. Please help me slow my pace long enough to enjoy all You have provided. Amen.

MARCH 1

When I grow up I want to be a little boy.
Joseph Heller

Lord, help me remember that childlike faith is what pleases You. Help me put aside all my sophisticated thoughts and theories and simply come to You as a child—full of faith and trust. Amen.

NOVEMBER 1

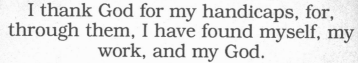

I thank God for my handicaps, for, through them, I have found myself, my work, and my God.

Helen Keller

Dear Father, sometimes it is so hard to see my handicaps as blessings. Help me see with Your eyes so that I might rejoice in who I am. And, more importantly, Lord, help me to know You better. Amen.

MARCH 2

Today are you trying to find out the future by consulting witches and mediums? Don't listen to their whisperings and mutterings. Can the living find out the future from the dead? Why not ask your God? Is. 8:19 TLB

Father, I will ask You. Please show me the Truth. I am sometimes confused by the world's answers and the world's confusion. Please protect me from being misled and misguided. Amen.

OCTOBER 31

Nobody can always have devout feelings;
and even if we could, feelings are not what
God principally cares about.
Christian, love...is an affair of the will.
But, the great feelings come and go, his
love for us does not.

C.S. Lewis

...cause of the Lord's great love we are not
...umed, for his compassions never

Lam. 3:22 NIV

MARCH 3

Do good with what thou hast, or it will do thee no good. Penn

Kindness makes a man attractive..
Prov. 19:22 TLB

Wisdom reposes in the heart of the discerning... Prov. 14:33 NIV

OCTOBER 30

God has promised forgiveness to your repentance; but He has not promised tomorrow to your procrastination.

St. Augustine

Thank You, Lord, for providing the strength to bear whatever the day may bring. Please help me to not leave for another day any task You would have me do today. Amen.

MARCH 4

No man ever sank under the burden of the day. It is when tomorrow's burden is added to the burden of today that the weight is more than a man can bear.

Macdonald.

Therefore do not worry about tomorrow, for tomorrow will worry about itself. Each day has enough trouble of its own.

Matt. 6:34 NIV

OCTOBER 29

Hardship is often God strengthening us.

Consider it pure joy, my brothers, whenever you face trials of many kinds, because you know that the testing of your faith develops perseverance. Perseverance must finish its work so that you may be mature and complete, not lacking anything. James 1:2-4 NIV

MARCH 5

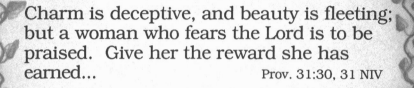

Charm is deceptive, and beauty is fleeting; but a woman who fears the Lord is to be praised. Give her the reward she has earned...

Prov. 31:30, 31 NIV

Father, thank You for the example of a godly woman that You have put in my life. Give me the strength to put into practice what I have learned at her knee. Amen.

OCTOBER 28

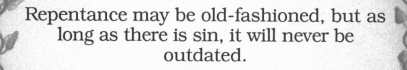

Repentance may be old-fashioned, but as long as there is sin, it will never be outdated.

If we confess our sins, he is faithful and just and will forgive us our sins and purify us from all unrighteousness.

1 John 1:9 NIV

MARCH 6

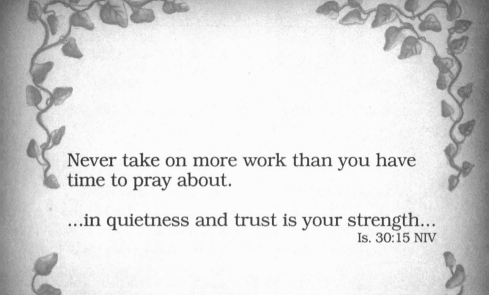

Never take on more work than you have time to pray about.

...in quietness and trust is your strength...
Is. 30:15 NIV

OCTOBER 27

Happiness is not the absence of conflict,
but the ability to deal with it.

A righteous man may have many
troubles, but the Lord delivers him from
them all.   Ps. 34:19 NIV

MARCH 7

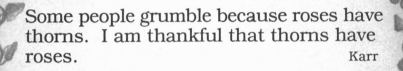

Some people grumble because roses have thorns. I am thankful that thorns have roses.   Karr

Father, help me keep this perspective on life; to look for Your grace and blessings in everything. Help me focus on thankfulness and learn not to complain. Amen.

OCTOBER 26

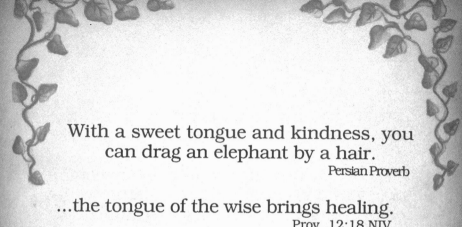

With a sweet tongue and kindness, you
can drag an elephant by a hair.

Persian Proverb

...the tongue of the wise brings healing.

Prov. 12:18 NIV

MARCH 8

To have what we want is riches; but to be able to do without, is power.   Macdonald

...I have learned the secret of being content in any and every situation, whether well fed or hungry... I can do everything through him who gives me strength.

Phil. 4:12 & 13 NIV

OCTOBER 25

The highest reward for a man's toil is not what he gets for it, but what he becomes by it.

John Ruskin

The sleep of a laborer is sweet, whether he eats little or much.

Ecc. 5:12 NIV

MARCH 9

Are you lonely, O my brother?
　　Share your little with another!
Stretch a hand to one unfriended,
　　And your loneliness is ended.

Teach my heart to reach out to others
and continually remind me, Father, that I
have many brothers and sisters in Your
family. Amen.

OCTOBER 24

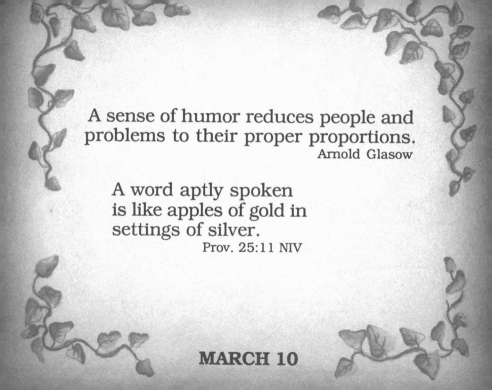

A sense of humor reduces people and
problems to their proper proportions.
Arnold Glasow

A word aptly spoken
is like apples of gold in
settings of silver.
Prov. 25:11 NIV

MARCH 10

A little learning is not a dangerous thing to one who does not mistake it for a great deal.   White

...let the wise listen and add to their learning and let the discerning get guidance——
The fear of the Lord is the beginning of knowledge...   Prov. 1:5 & 7 NIV

OCTOBER 23

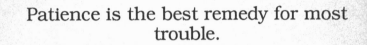

Patience is the best remedy for most trouble.

It is not good to have zeal without knowledge, nor to be hasty and miss the way.

Prov. 19:2 NIV

MARCH 11

When love and skill work together, expect a masterpiece.

Ruskin

Father, I give You my life and ask You to use Your love and Your skill to work a masterpiece in me. I confess to You that I fail when I try to go alone. Please take control of my life. Amen.

OCTOBER 22

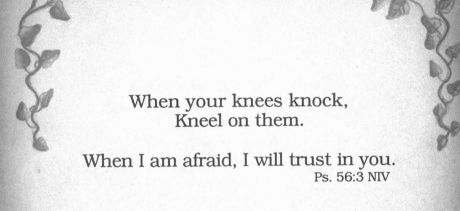

When your knees knock,
Kneel on them.

When I am afraid, I will trust in you.
Ps. 56:3 NIV

MARCH 12

One can live in the shadow of an idea without grasping it.   Elizabeth Bowen

I write these things to you who believe in the name of the Son of God so that you may know that you have eternal life.

I John 5:13 NIV

OCTOBER 21

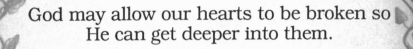

God may allow our hearts to be broken so
He can get deeper into them.

For though he wounds, he binds and
heals again. He will deliver you again and
again, so that no evil can touch you.

Job 5:18 & 19 TLB

MARCH 13

A learned man always has a wealth within himself.

I have hidden your word in my heart that I might not sin against you...
Teach me knowledge and good judgment, for I believe your commands...

Ps. 119:11 & 66 NIV

OCTOBER 20

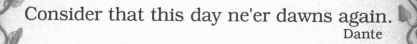

Consider that this day ne'er dawns again.
Dante

It is harder to see today when we are
looking at tomorrow.

"From this day on I will bless you."
Hagg. 2:19b NIV

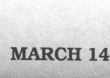

MARCH 14

If I had a single flower for everytime I think about you, I could walk forever in my garden.

Claudia Grandi

Thank You, Father, for my precious friend, a gift from You— someone with whom to share my joys and defeats, and a love centered in You. Amen.

OCTOBER 19

Discontentment makes rich men poor while contentment makes poor men rich.

...and be content with what you have, because God has said,
"Never will I leave you; Never will I forsake you." Heb. 13:5 NIV

MARCH 15

It is very helpful to make a habit of offering, morning by morning, the troubles of the day just beginning to our dear Lord, accepting His will in all things, especially in all little personal trials and vexations.

H.L. Lear

Though I walk in the midst of trouble, you preserve my life... Ps. 138:7 NIV

OCTOBER 18

You may say to yourself, "My power and the strength of my hands have produced this wealth for me."

But remember the Lord your God, for it is he who gives you the ability to produce wealth...

Deut. 8:17 & 18 NIV

I pray that I will never lose sight of this truth, Lord. All I have comes from You. Help me to hold all I have very lightly and may I always be ready to pass it along at Your request. Amen.

MARCH 16

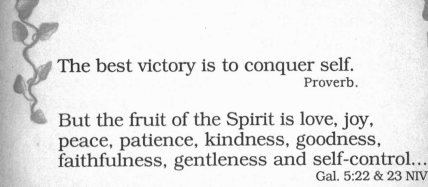

The best victory is to conquer self.
Proverb.

But the fruit of the Spirit is love, joy, peace, patience, kindness, goodness, faithfulness, gentleness and self-control...
Gal. 5:22 & 23 NIV

OCTOBER 17

We cannot shine if we have not taken time to fill our lamps.

For you were once darkness, but now you are light in the Lord. Live as children of light...nothing to do with the fruitless deeds of darkness...   Eph. 5:8-11 NIV

MARCH 17

It's easy to hate an enemy but it costs to love him!!

But love your enemies, do good to them, and tend to them without expecting to get anything back. Then your reward will be great.

Luke 6:35 NIV

OCTOBER 16

To stay young in spirit, keep taking on new thoughts and throwing off old habits.

Even in old age they will still produce fruit and be vital.

Ps. 92:14 TLB

MARCH 18

"I see Jesus in every human being. I say to myself, this is hungry Jesus, I must feed him. This is sick Jesus. This one has leprosy or gangrene; I must wash him and tend to him. I serve them because I love Jesus."

Mother Teresa

Remind me, Lord, that to get nearer to You I must care about others. Please help me see You when I look at those in need, and give me the desire to be a servant in Your strength. Amen.

OCTOBER 15

The real measure of a man's wealth is
what he has invested in eternity.

Do not store up for yourselves treasures
on earth, where moth and rust
destroy...But store up for yourselves
treasures in heaven...For where your
treasure is, there your heart will be also.

Matt. 6:19-21 NIV

MARCH 19

Those who have known a problem first hand are usually better able to help others walking through the same difficulty.

Praise be to the God and Father of our Lord Jesus Christ, the Father of compassion and the God of all comfort, who comforts us in all our troubles, so that we can comfort those in any trouble with the comfort we ourselves have received from God.   II Cor. 1:3 & 4 NIV

OCTOBER 14

Every person in this world is a dream of God.

Then God said,"Let us make man in our image, in our likeness...". So God created man in his own image, in the image of God he created him; male and female he created them. God blessed them.

Gen. 1:26-28 NIV

MARCH 20

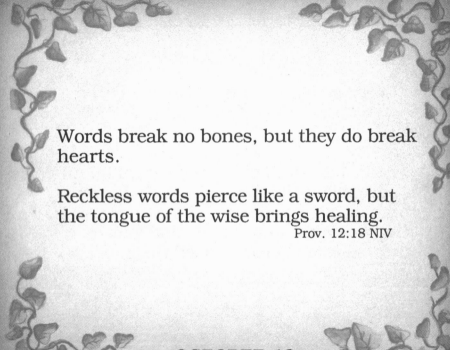

Words break no bones, but they do break hearts.

Reckless words pierce like a sword, but the tongue of the wise brings healing.

Prov. 12:18 NIV

OCTOBER 13

When you get to the end of your rope, tie a knot and hang on...

...we do not lose heart... Our...troubles are achieving for us an eternal glory that far outweighs them all. So we fix our eyes not on what is seen, but what is unseen. For what is seen is temporary, but what is unseen is eternal.   II Cor. 4:16 & 17 NIV

MARCH 21

Worry is wasting today's time to clutter up tomorrow's opportunities with yesterday's troubles!!

Therefore, do not worry about tomorrow, for tomorrow will worry about itself. Each day has enough trouble of its own.

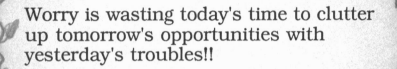

Matt. 6:34 NIV

OCTOBER 12

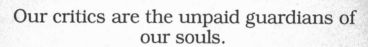

Our critics are the unpaid guardians of our souls.

Ten Boom

Better is open rebuke than hidden love. Wounds from a friend can be trusted...

Prov. 27:5 & 6 NIV

MARCH 22

Last eve I saw a beauty contest brief
Between a rainbow and an autumn leaf.

The message of the leaves in their cycles
from bud to green to red to brown is that
we should experience everything in its
season.

*Father, help me accept the stages of life
as part of Your plan. May I learn to rest
in this and every "season" and to enjoy
it fully. Amen.*

OCTOBER 11

Sometimes my conversations with God sound as if I am using a phone without a receiver— only a mouthpiece!

...Speak, Lord, for your servant is listening

I Sam. 3:9 NIV

Lord, please give me grace and wisdom to know when to speak and when to remain silent. Amen.

MARCH 23

I long to accomplish great and noble tasks, but it is my chief duty and joy to accomplish humble tasks as though they were great and noble. Helen Keller

Dear Heavenly Father, I am so thankful for Your loving care. You are interested in everything that I do and say. Your provisions are sufficient for all my needs. Keep me ever aware that I am Your child. Amen.

OCTOBER 10

I know that my Redeemer lives and that in the end He will stand upon the earth. I myself will see Him with my own eyes—I, and not another. How my heart yearns within me!

Job 19:25 & 27 NIV

Oh, Lord, may my love for You be evident in the labor of my hands and in my defense of justice and goodness. Amen.

MARCH 24

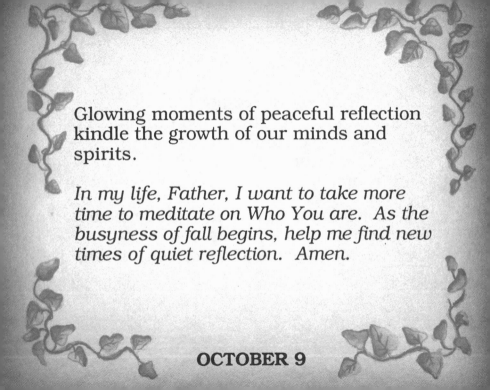

Glowing moments of peaceful reflection kindle the growth of our minds and spirits.

In my life, Father, I want to take more time to meditate on Who You are. As the busyness of fall begins, help me find new times of quiet reflection. Amen.

OCTOBER 9

The great Easter truth is not that we are to live newly after death— that is not the great thing— but that we are to be new here and now by the power of the resurrection...

Brooks

Therefore, if anyone is in Christ, he is a new creation; the old has gone, the new has come! All this is from God...

II Cor. 5:17 &18 NIV

MARCH 25

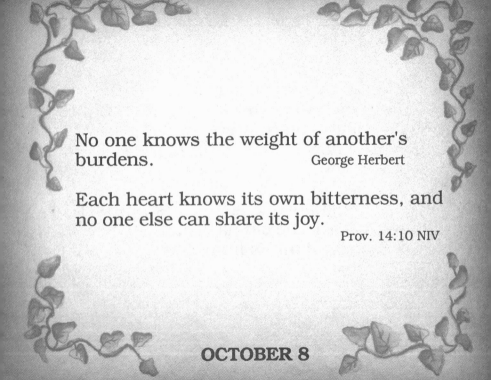

No one knows the weight of another's
burdens.   George Herbert

Each heart knows its own bitterness, and
no one else can share its joy.
                                    Prov. 14:10 NIV

OCTOBER 8

Worship is the highway of reverence and washes the dust of earth from our eyes.

Worship the Lord with gladness; come before him with joyful songs...For the Lord is good and his love endures forever; his faithfulness continues through all generations. Ps. 100:2 & 5 NIV

MARCH 26

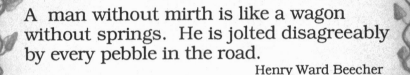

A man without mirth is like a wagon without springs. He is jolted disagreeably by every pebble in the road.

Henry Ward Beecher

A man finds joy in giving an apt reply, and how good is a timely word!

Prov. 15:23 NIV

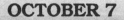

OCTOBER 7

A good exercise for the heart is to bend
down and help another up.

And we urge you, brothers...help the
weak...always try to be kind to each
other...   I Thess. 5:14 & 15 NIV

MARCH 27

Worry often gives a small thing a big shadow.
Swedish Proverb

How often I crouch in the shadow of worry, Lord, instead of walking in Your light. Help me learn to pray about concerns instead of worrying about them. Amen.

OCTOBER 6

Thy part is to yield thyself,
His part is to work; and never, never will
He give thee any command which is not
accompanied by ample power to obey it.
                                    Hannah Whitall Smith

We do not know what to do, but our eyes
are upon you.   II Chron. 20:12b NIV

*How often I look at the work to be done
instead of at You, Father. Help me keep
my eyes on You. Amen.*

MARCH 28

To enjoy the things we ought and to hate the things we ought has the greatest bearing on excellence of character.

Aristotle

If you are wise, your wisdom will reward you.

Prov. 9:12 NIV

OCTOBER 5

There is comfort in the fact that God can never be taken by surprise.

Gabelein

For the eyes of the Lord range throughout the earth to strengthen those whose hearts are fully committed to him. II Chron. 16:9 NIV

MARCH 29

Shall we accept good from God and not trouble? In all this, Job did not sin in what he said.   Job 2:10 NIV

Father, You know how often I'm tempted to blame You. Please give me Job's wisdom and help me understand that nothing comes to me that doesn't first pass through Your hand. Amen.

OCTOBER 4

Don't let the abundance of God's gifts
cause you to forget the Giver.

Oh, the depth of the riches of the wisdom
and knowledge of God!   Rom. 11:33 NIV

MARCH 30

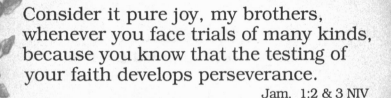

Consider it pure joy, my brothers, whenever you face trials of many kinds, because you know that the testing of your faith develops perseverance.

Jam. 1:2 & 3 NIV

Lord, give me the wisdom to make stepping stones out of stumbling blocks. Amen.

OCTOBER 3

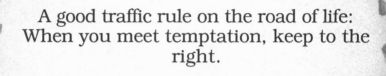

A good traffic rule on the road of life:
When you meet temptation, keep to the
right.

Do not set foot on the path of the wicked
or walk in the way of evil men...turn from
it and go on your way.   Prov. 4:14 & 15 NIV

MARCH 31

Take care of the world, lest it unawares
steals away your heart.

Susanna Wesley

So, give yourselves humbly to God. Resist
the devil and he will flee from you...draw
close to God, God will draw close to you...

Jam. 4:7 & 8 TLB

OCTOBER 2

When God measures a person He puts the tape around his heart and not his head.

As water reflects a face, so a man's heart reflects the man.   Prov. 27:19 NIV

All a man's ways seem right to him, but the Lord weighs the heart. To do what is right and just is more acceptable to the Lord than sacrifice.   Prov. 21:2 & 3 NIV

APRIL 1

God made you as you are in order to use you as he planned. S.C. McAuley

Thank You for reminding me that I am fearfully and wonderfully made. Please give me the grace to rejoice in who I am, and to surrender myself, just as I am, to You. Amen.

OCTOBER 1

Though you may ask God to do something <u>for</u> you,
He generally wants to do something <u>in</u> you.

Search me, O God, and know my heart; test me and know my anxious thoughts. See if there is any offensive way in me, and lead me in the way everlasting.

Ps. 139:23 & 24 NIV

APRIL 2

Things are not to be done by the effort of the moment, but by the preparation of past moments. Cecil

I ask for Your instruction in my life, Father, that I might meet each moment with sufficient preparation to stand strong in You. Amen.

SEPTEMBER 30

Courage for the great sorrows of life, and patience for the small ones, and when you have laboriously accomplished your daily task, go to sleep in peace.

God is awake.
Victor Hugo

Thank You, Father, for the wonderful knowledge that You, our Provider, never sleep nor slumber. You, the mighty Creator of the universe, love and protect me. Amen.

APRIL 3

I still find each day too short for all the thoughts I want to think, all the walks I want to take, all the books I want to read, and all the friends I want to see.

Burroughs

Lord, thank You for the love of life that You have put within me. Help me make wise choices this day as I have the privilege of choosing how to spend an hour. May I do all to Your glory. Amen.

SEPTEMBER 29

Wherever a man or a woman turns he can find someone who needs him.
 Even if it is a little thing— do something for which there is no pay— but the privilege of just doing it.
Remember, you don't live in the world all on your own.

Albert Schweitzer

Father, there is so much need and so little time. Please give me the desire and strength to reach out to others in Your name. Amen.

APRIL 4

Daily duties are daily joys, because they are something which God gives us to offer unto Him, to do to our very best, in acknowledgement of His love.

Pusey

Sometimes my life seems so dreary and the sameness of my days is discouraging. Thank You for a new vision and encouragement to serve You right where I am. Amen.

SEPTEMBER 28

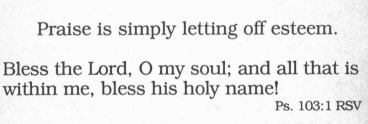

Praise is simply letting off esteem.

Bless the Lord, O my soul; and all that is within me, bless his holy name!

Ps. 103:1 RSV

APRIL 5

When we see not our way through some trial or difficulty, we have only to look to God, and to wait in patience, and in due time His light will come and guide us.

Ullathorne

I wait for the Lord, my soul waits, and in his word I put my hope. My soul waits for the Lord.

Ps. 130:5 & 6 NIV

SEPTEMBER 27

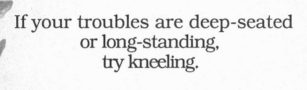

If your troubles are deep-seated
        or long-standing,
            try kneeling.

Is any one of you in trouble? He should
pray. Is anyone happy? Let him sing
songs of praise.

James 5:13 NIV

APRIL 6

I'm wishing at this very time that I could but repay a portion of the gladness that you've strewn along my way. And if I could have one wish this year, this only would it be: I'd like to be the sort of friend that you have been to me.   Guest

What a friend we have in Jesus.
                                    Converse

SEPTEMBER 26

Four things to learn in life:
To think clearly without hurry or
    confusion;
To love everybody sincerely;
To act in everything with the highest
    motives;
To trust God unhesitatingly.

Helen Keller

But seek first his kingdom and his
righteousness, and all these things shall
be yours as well.   Matt. 6:33 RSV

APRIL 7

Worry is a thin stream of fear trickling through the mind. If encouraged, it cuts a channel into which all other thoughts are drained.

A.S. Roche

When worry fills my mind and anxious thoughts grip my heart, please give me the strength to turn my thoughts to You, Lord. To remember that You control the future and are caring for me is the channel into which I want my thoughts to flow. Amen.

SEPTEMBER 25

Our Lord has written the promise of the resurrection not in books alone, but in every leaf in the springtime.

Martin Luther

In every plant, in every flower, I see the wonder of Your creation. Thank You for the promise of Spring...the hope of new life. Amen.

APRIL 8

I find that it is not the circumstances in which we are placed, but the spirit in which we meet them that constitutes our comfort...

Elizabeth King

When I am afraid, I will trust in you. In God, in whose word I praise, in God I trust; I will not be afraid...

Ps. 56:3 & 4 NIV

SEPTEMBER 24

No man or company of men, no power on earth or heaven can touch that soul which is abiding in Christ without first passing through His encircling presence and receiving the seal of His permission. If God be for us, it matters not who may be against us; nothing can disturb or harm us, except He shall see it is best for us.

Hannah Whitall Smith

For the faith and confidence that comes from walking with You daily, Lord, I give You thanks. You have taught me Your faithfulness in the easy times so I can trust You in the hard times. Amen.

APRIL 9

The angel fetched Peter out of prison, but it was prayer that fetched the angel.

Thomas Watson

Call to me and I will answer you...

Jer. 33:3 NIV

Thank You for this promise, Lord—how wonderful that we can call on You and You promise to answer. Amen.

SEPTEMBER 23

Afflictions may be lasting, but not everlasting.

Watson

Be joyful in hope, patient in affliction, faithful in prayer.

Romans 12:12 NIV

APRIL 10

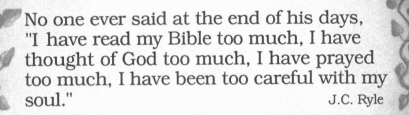

No one ever said at the end of his days, "I have read my Bible too much, I have thought of God too much, I have prayed too much, I have been too careful with my soul."

J.C. Ryle

Blessed are they who keep his statutes and seek him with all their hearts...they walk in his ways.

Ps. 119:2 & 3 NIV

SEPTEMBER 22

The dewdrop fulfills the Lord's will as much as the thunderstorm.

Are not two sparrows sold for a penny? Yet not one of them will fall to the ground apart from the will of your Father. And even the very hairs of your head are numbered. So, don't be afraid; you are worth more than many sparrows.

Matt. 10:29 & 31 NIV

APRIL 11

One of the first things which a physician says to his patients is, "Let me see your tongue." A spiritual advisor might ask the same thing.

N. Adams

...he who holds his tongue is wise.

Prov. 10:19 NIV

SEPTEMBER 21

Although salvation is a free gift we sometimes forget that we still must ask for it.

For God so loved the world that he gave his one and only Son, that whoever believes in him shall not perish but have eternal life.

John 3:16 NIV

APRIL 12

Full grown oaks are not produced in three years; neither are servants of God.

Douglas Rumford

Father, it's hard not to grow weary as I strive to be a servant. Help me rely on You for strength and not on my own power. Thank you that You will work through me and I don't have to strive in my own strength. Amen.

SEPTEMBER 20

The refiner is never very far from the mouth of the furnace when his gold is in the fire.   C.H.Spurgeon

"...I will refine them like silver and test them like gold. They will call on my name and I will answer them; I will say, 'They are my people' and they will say, 'The Lord is our God.' "   Zech. 13:9 NIV

APRIL 13

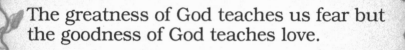

The greatness of God teaches us fear but the goodness of God teaches love.

Every good and perfect gift is from above, coming down from the Father of the heavenly lights... James 1:17 NIV

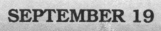

SEPTEMBER 19

We make our decisions and often our decisions then make us.

Dear Lord, I sometimes forget that decisions I make today have far-reaching influence. Please direct my path and help me be willing to have You involved in every decision that I make. Amen.

APRIL 14

Never lose sight of the fact that old age needs so little, but it needs that little so much.

Margaret Willour

...love one another. As I have loved you so you must love one another.

John 13:34 NIV

SEPTEMBER 18

Jesus said:
"Do not let your hearts be troubled. Trust in God; trust also in me. In my Father's house are many rooms; if it were not so, I would have told you. I am going there to prepare a place for you. And if I go and prepare a place for you, I will come back and take you to be with me that you also may be where I am. John 14:1-3 NIV

APRIL 15

Consider what God has done:

Who can straighten
   what He has made crooked:
When times are good, be happy;
   but when times are bad, consider:
God has made the one
   as well as the other.

Ecc. 7:13 & 14 NIV

SEPTEMBER 17

Our object in life should not be so much to get through a great deal of work, as to give perfect satisfaction to Him for whom we are doing the work.   Aitken

It is the Lord your God you must follow, and him you must revere.   Deut. 13:4 NIV

APRIL 16

May you always be doing those good kind things which show that you are a child of God, for this will bring much praise and glory to God.

Phil. 1:11 TLB

How exciting to think that I can bring glory to You, Father. Please give me the energy and strength to do the things that are important to You. Amen.

SEPTEMBER 16

No one can make you feel inferior without your consent.

Eleanor Roosevelt

You do not have because you do not ask...Submit yourselves, then, to God. Resist the devil, and he will flee from you. Come near to God and he will come near to you.

James 4:2, 7 & 8 NIV

APRIL 17

We would be more grateful if we knew how much of what we take for granted is planned by God!

Forgive me for taking Your loving care for granted. You provide for me in such loving ways and I am often too busy to notice. Thank you for the evidence of Your hand in my life. Amen.

SEPTEMBER 15

Pray for a good harvest, but keep on hoeing.

The man who plants and the man who waters have one purpose, and each will be rewarded according to his own labor. For we are God's fellow workers...

I Cor. 3: 8 & 9 NIV

APRIL 18

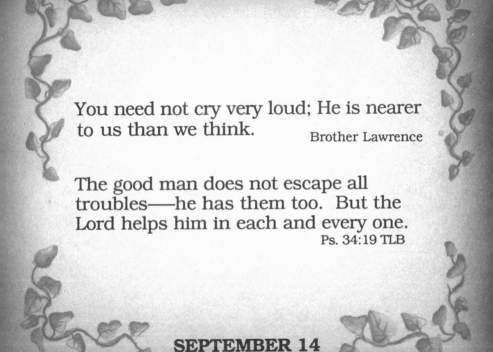

You need not cry very loud; He is nearer
to us than we think.   Brother Lawrence

The good man does not escape all
troubles——he has them too. But the
Lord helps him in each and every one.
                                    Ps. 34:19 TLB

SEPTEMBER 14

A Christian does not own his wealth; he owes it.

Give, and it will be given to you... For with the measure you use, it will be measured to you.

Luke 6:38 NIV

APRIL 19

As long as the earth remains, there will be springtime and harvest, cold and heat, winter and summer, day and night.

Gen. 8:22 TLB

...Great is Your faithfulness!

SEPTEMBER 13

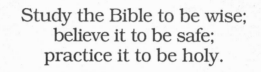

Study the Bible to be wise;
believe it to be safe;
practice it to be holy.

Oh, how I love your law! I meditate on it all
day long. Your commands make me wiser
than my enemies.

Ps. 119:97 & 98 NIv

APRIL 20

A search for wisdom without God ends in deception.

If any of you lacks wisdom, he should ask God, who gives generously to all without finding fault, and it will be given to him. But when he asks, he must believe...

James 1:5 & 6 NIV

SEPTEMBER 12

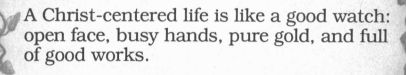

A Christ-centered life is like a good watch: open face, busy hands, pure gold, and full of good works.

Do not be overcome by evil, but overcome evil with good.   Rom. 12:21 NIV

APRIL 21

The fear of God is the soul of Godliness.
John Murray

If you, O Lord, kept a record of sins,
O Lord, who could stand?
But with you there is forgiveness;
therefore you are feared.
Ps. 130:3 & 4 NIV

SEPTEMBER 11

May our Lord Jesus Christ himself and God our Father, who loved us and by his grace gave us eternal encouragement and good hope, encourage your hearts and strengthen you in every good deed and word.　　　　II Thes. 2:16 NIV

Thank You, Father, for this promise of Your steadfast love. I am so thankful that no situation I face is too difficult if You are with me. Give me the faith to persevere. Amen.

APRIL 22

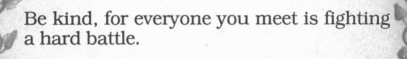

Be kind, for everyone you meet is fighting a hard battle.

Thank You for reminding me that others walk uphill just as I do. How often I forget and think that I walk hardship's path alone. Amen.

SEPTEMBER 10

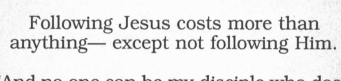

Following Jesus costs more than anything— except not following Him.

"And no one can be my disciple who does not carry his own cross and follow me. But don't begin until you count the cost..."

Luke 14:27 & 28 TLB

APRIL 23

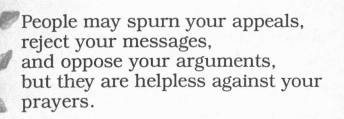

People may spurn your appeals,
reject your messages,
and oppose your arguments,
but they are helpless against your
prayers.

...in everything, by prayer and petition,
with thanksgiving, present your requests
to God.   Phil 4:6 NIV

SEPTEMBER 9

A life watered by the tears of tragedy and suffering often becomes the most fertile soil for spiritual growth.

"You intended to harm me, but God intended it for good to accomplish what is now being done..." Gen. 50:20 NIV

APRIL 24

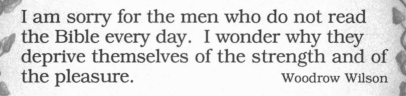

I am sorry for the men who do not read the Bible every day. I wonder why they deprive themselves of the strength and of the pleasure. Woodrow Wilson

...I have put my hope in your Word. I know, O Lord, that your laws are righteous. Ps. 119:74 & 75 NIV

SEPTEMBER 8

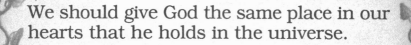

We should give God the same place in our hearts that he holds in the universe.

The earth is the Lord's and everything in it: the world, and all who live in it; for he founded it upon the seas and established it upon the waters.

Ps. 24: 1 & 2 NIV

APRIL 25

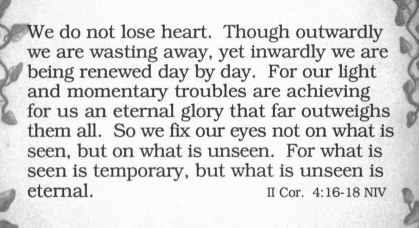

We do not lose heart. Though outwardly we are wasting away, yet inwardly we are being renewed day by day. For our light and momentary troubles are achieving for us an eternal glory that far outweighs them all. So we fix our eyes not on what is seen, but on what is unseen. For what is seen is temporary, but what is unseen is eternal.

II Cor. 4:16-18 NIV

SEPTEMBER 7

If you live close to God
and His infinite grace,
You don't have to tell
it shows on your face.

Change me inside, Lord, so that my life
will be a witness to Your transforming
power. Amen.

APRIL 26

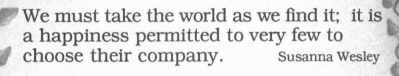

We must take the world as we find it; it is a happiness permitted to very few to choose their company.   Susanna Wesley

Walk in all the way that the Lord your God has commanded you, so that you may live and prosper and prolong your days in the land that you possess.

Deut. 5:33 NIV

SEPTEMBER 6

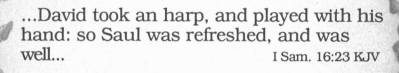

...David took an harp, and played with his hand: so Saul was refreshed, and was well...

I Sam. 16:23 KJV

Teach me, Lord, to serve others instead of serving myself. Help me learn that love grows from giving. Amen.

APRIL 27

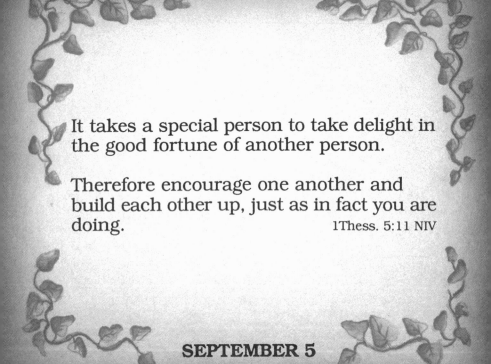

It takes a special person to take delight in the good fortune of another person.

Therefore encourage one another and build each other up, just as in fact you are doing.

1Thess. 5:11 NIV

SEPTEMBER 5

Be very sensitive to your benefactors, no matter how small their gifts in your behalf.
Don't let any kindness go unappreciated.

Thank you, Lord, for Your blessings in my life — great and small. My heart is full as I remember them all, especially the wonderful gift of Your Son. Amen.

Thanks be to God for his indescribable gift!

II Cor. 9:15 NIV

APRIL 28

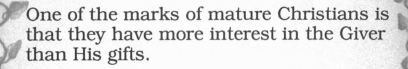

One of the marks of mature Christians is that they have more interest in the Giver than His gifts.

...set your hearts on things above, where Christ is seated at the right hand of God. Set your mind on things above, not on earthly things. Col. 3:1 & 2 NIV

SEPTEMBER 4

When someone does you wrong, don't do what comes naturally; do what comes supernaturally— Love him.

You know this is impossible for me to do this without Your help, Lord. Give me a spirit of love and teach me to let Your love flow through me. Amen.

APRIL 29

"Naked I came from my mother's womb and naked I will depart. The Lord gave and the Lord has taken away; may the name of the Lord be praised." In all this Job did not sin by charging God with wrong doing.   Job 1:21 & 22 NIV

Father, please give me the grace to praise You in all circumstances——to not question Your wisdom or to grow bitter. It is so difficult, especially when uncertainty plagues my path. Amen.

SEPTEMBER 3

Spring cleaning should begin with the head and end with the heart.

Search me, O God, and know my heart, test me and know my anxious thoughts. See if there is any offensive way in me, and lead me in the way everlasting.

Ps. 139:23 & 24 NIV

APRIL 30

We keep the best of that which we give away.

You know the grace of our Lord Jesus Christ, that though he was rich, yet for your sakes he became poor, so that you through his poverty might become rich.

II Cor. 8:9 NIV

SEPTEMBER 2

There is no better exercise for strengthening the heart than reaching down and lifting up another.

Lord, please use me to lift others up even as You have sent others to lift me in my times of need. Amen.

MAY 1

I have read in Plato and Cicero sayings that are very wise and very beautiful; but I never read in either of them, "Come unto me all ye that labor and are heavy laden and I will give you rest." Augustine

The wisdom of the ages is nothing when compared to Your promises, Lord. How we all yearn for rest and it is ours for the asking. Amen.

SEPTEMBER 1

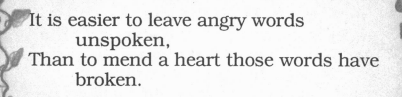

It is easier to leave angry words
        unspoken,
Than to mend a heart those words have
        broken.

A gentle answer turns away wrath, but a
harsh word stirs up anger.

Prov. 15:1 NIV

MAY 2

Whether seventy or sixteen, there is in every being's heart the love of wonder, the sweet amazement at the stars and the starlike things and thoughts, the undaunted challenge of events, the unfailing childlike appetite for what next, and the joy and the game of life.

Anonymous

But it is the spirit in a man, the breath of the Almighty, that gives him understanding.

Job 32:8 NIV

AUGUST 31

Acknowledge and take to heart this day that the Lord is God in heaven above and on the earth below. There is no other. Keep his decrees and commands...so that it may go well with you and your children after you and that you may live long...

Deut. 4:39 & 40 NIV

Father, in this world of distractions, help me surrender the foolish and vain idols I put before You. Amen.

MAY 3

If there be some weaker one,
Give me strength to help him on;
If a blinder soul there be,
Let me guide him nearer Thee;
Make my mortal dreams come true
With the work I fain would do;
Clothe with life the weak intent,
Let me be the thing I meant;
Let me find in Thy employ,
Peace that dearer is than joy;
Out of self to love be led,
And to heaven acclimated
Until all things sweet and good
Seem my natural habitude.

Whittier

AUGUST 30

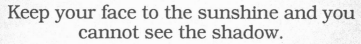

Keep your face to the sunshine and you
cannot see the shadow.

Helen Keller

There is no shadow, Lord, if I place myself
directly in the sunshine of Your presence.
Thank You. Amen.

MAY 4

Whatever is to make us better and happy, God has placed either openly before us or close to us.   Seneca

The Word became flesh and lived for a while among us.   John 1:14 NIV

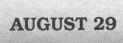

AUGUST 29

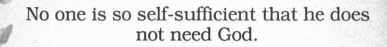

No one is so self-sufficient that he does not need God.

Father, help me to see my need for You. Teach me to lean on You and Your wisdom and not the world and its wisdom. Amen.

MAY 5

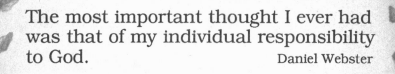

The most important thought I ever had was that of my individual responsibility to God. Daniel Webster

...to all who received him, to those who believed in his name, he gave the right to become children of God.

John 1:12 NIV

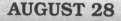

AUGUST 28

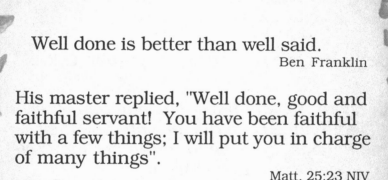

Well done is better than well said.

Ben Franklin

His master replied, "Well done, good and faithful servant! You have been faithful with a few things; I will put you in charge of many things".

Matt. 25:23 NIV

MAY 6

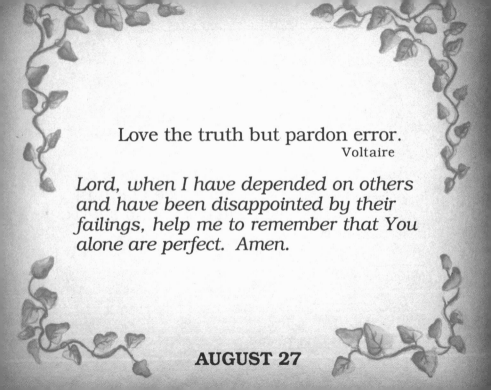

Love the truth but pardon error.
Voltaire

Lord, when I have depended on others and have been disappointed by their failings, help me to remember that You alone are perfect. Amen.

AUGUST 27

If you find a path with no obstacles, it probably doesn't lead anywhere.

Lord, help me to see obstacles as stepping stones on the path to greater dependence on You. Amen.

MAY 7

To awaken each morning with a smile brightening my face; to approach my work with a clean mind; to hold ever before me, the Ultimate Purpose toward which I am working; to meet men and women with laughter on my lips and love in my heart; to be gentle, kind, and courteous through all the hours; to approach the night with weariness that ever woos sleep and the joy that comes from work well done—— this is how I desire to waste wisely my days.

Dekker

AUGUST 26

It is one thing to go through a crisis grandly, but another thing to go through every day glorifying God when there is no witness, no limelight, no one paying the remotest attention to us.

Oswald Chambers

In every part of every day I thank You for walking beside me. Thank You for the joy that Your closeness brings. Amen.

MAY 8

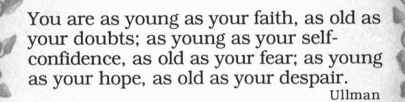

You are as young as your faith, as old as your doubts; as young as your self-confidence, as old as your fear; as young as your hope, as old as your despair.

Ullman

It is not only the old who are wise, nor only the aged who understand what is right.

Job 32:9 NIV

AUGUST 25

It is easier to see another person's deceit than your own.

Arthur Dobrin

...first take the plank out of your own eye, and then you will see clearly to remove the speck from your brother's eye.

Matt. 7:5 NIV

MAY 9

Prayer is a preparation for danger,
it is the armor for battle. Go not into the
dangerous world without it.

Robertson

...be constant in prayer
Rom. 12:12 RSV

AUGUST 24

Obedience belongs to us;
results belong to God.

If you fully obey the Lord your God and
carefully follow all his commands I give
you today, the Lord your God will set you
high above all the nations on earth. All
these blessings will come upon you and
accompany you if you obey the Lord your
God.

Deut. 28:1 & 2 NIV

MAY 10

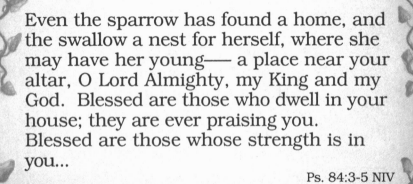

Even the sparrow has found a home, and the swallow a nest for herself, where she may have her young—— a place near your altar, O Lord Almighty, my King and my God. Blessed are those who dwell in your house; they are ever praising you.
Blessed are those whose strength is in you...

Ps. 84:3-5 NIV

AUGUST 23

Yielding to the will of God is not bondage–
it is blessing.

Commit your way to the Lord; trust in
him and he will do this: He will make your
righteousness shine like the dawn, the
justice of your cause like the noonday
sun.

Ps. 37:5 & 6 NIV

MAY 11

Do not be anxious about anything, but in everything by prayer and petition , with thanksgiving, present your requests to God. And the peace of God, which transcends all understanding, will guard your hearts and minds in Christ Jesus. Finally, brothers, whatever is true, whatever is noble, whatever is right, whatever is pure, whatever is lovely, whatever is admirable—— if anything is excellent or praiseworthy—— think about such things.

Phil 4:6-8 NIV

AUGUST 22

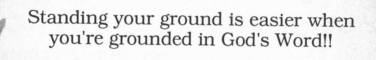

Standing your ground is easier when
you're grounded in God's Word!!

I have hidden your word in my heart that
I might not sin against you.

Ps. 119:11 NIV

MAY 12

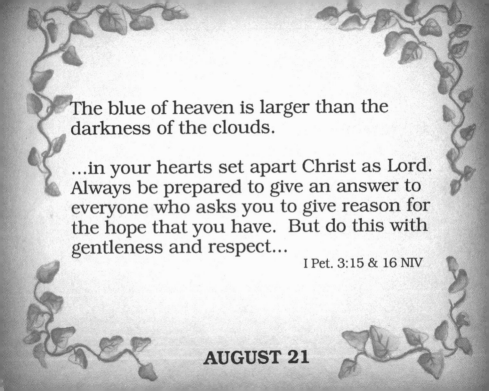

The blue of heaven is larger than the darkness of the clouds.

...in your hearts set apart Christ as Lord. Always be prepared to give an answer to everyone who asks you to give reason for the hope that you have. But do this with gentleness and respect...

I Pet. 3:15 & 16 NIV

AUGUST 21

Amazing isn't it how some people see the basket half empty and others see it half full.

Some see life hopeless; others hopeful. Even when things are less than perfect, if you can think of the good, the beautiful, the hopeful, you'll be more than sustained—you'll conquer.

...whatever is true, ...whatever is right, whatever is pure, whatever is lovely,... think about such things...put it into practice. And the God of peace will be with you. Phil. 4:8 & 9 NIV

MAY 13

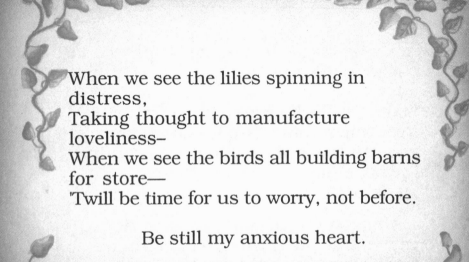

When we see the lilies spinning in
distress,
Taking thought to manufacture
loveliness–
When we see the birds all building barns
for store—
'Twill be time for us to worry, not before.

Be still my anxious heart.

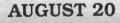

AUGUST 20

There are many shadows, but remember, where there is a shadow there must be a light.

Jesus is the light --
He's the light of the world.

MAY 14

What sunshine is to flowers, smiles are to humanity. They are but trifles, to be sure; but, scattered along life's pathway, the good they do is inconceivable.

Addison

The light of the righteous shines brightly...

Prov. 13:9 NIV

AUGUST 19

It isn't the load that weighs us down --
it's the way we carry it.

My grace is sufficient for you, for my
power is made perfect in weakness.

II Cor. 12:9 NIV

*Thank You for this promise, Lord. I need
to be reminded of Your power because it is
so hard to keep my eyes off my weakness.
Help me remember that Your grace is
sufficient. Amen.*

MAY 15

...the gift of God is eternal life through Christ Jesus our Lord.

Rom. 6:23 NIV

You were shown these things so that you might know that the Lord is God; besides him there is no other.

Deut. 4:35 NIV

AUGUST 18

That we are alive today is proof positive
that God has something for us to do
today.

Lindsay

Let us then approach the throne of grace
with confidence, so that we may receive
mercy and find grace to help us in our
time of need.

Heb. 4:16 NIV

MAY 16

No man is poor who has had a Godly mother. Abraham Lincoln

Charm is deceptive, and beauty is fleeting; but a woman who fears the Lord is to be praised. Prov. 31:30 NIV

AUGUST 17

He who plants a garden works hand in hand with God.

Malloch

Lord, teach me to plant the seeds that help meet the needs of others and to remember that it is You who blesses the work of my hands. Amen.

I planted the seed, Apollos watered it, but God made it grow.

I Cor. 3:6 NIV

MAY 17

To know where you can find a thing is in reality the best part of learning.

I have hidden your word in my heart...your statutes are my delight; they are my counselors...your word is a lamp to my feet and a light for my path...I have put my hope in your word...Great peace have they who love your law, and nothing can make them stumble. Ps. 119 NIV

AUGUST 16

As the blossom cannot tell what becomes of its fragrance, so, no one can tell what becomes of his influence.

Make me aware, Lord, that today never returns. May the sweet fragrance of Your loving kindness follow me through this day. Amen.

MAY 18

Never deliberate about what is clearly wrong, and try to persuade yourself that it is not. Frederick Temple

Follow justice and justice alone, so that you may live... Deut. 16:20 NIV

AUGUST 15

If it's more precious to you than God,
spell it I-D-O-L.

*Lord, give me the courage to part with
what I hold most dear, if it separates me
from You.
Please put into my heart the right desires
and a thirst for You. Amen.*

MAY 19

Our duty is not to see through one another, but to see one another through.

Carry each other's burdens, and in this way you will fulfill the law of Christ.

Gal. 6:2 NIV

AUGUST 14

The Christian ideal has not been tried
and found wanting.
It has been found difficult and left untried.

Chesterton

O Lord, be gracious to us;
we long for you.
Be our strength every morning,
our salvation in time of distress.

Is. 33:2 NIV

MAY 20

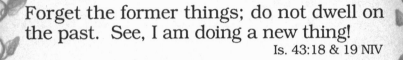

Forget the former things; do not dwell on the past. See, I am doing a new thing!

Is. 43:18 & 19 NIV

Thank You, Lord, for this promise. I am discouraged and find myself looking backward instead of to the future. Help me see the "new thing" You are doing in my life. Amen.

AUGUST 13

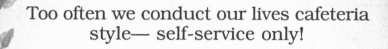

Too often we conduct our lives cafeteria style— self-service only!

...whoever wants to be first must be slave of all. For even the Son of Man did not come to be served, but to serve...

Mark 10:44 & 45 NIV

MAY 21

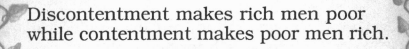

Discontentment makes rich men poor
while contentment makes poor men rich.

...be content with what you have, because
God has said,
"Never will I leave you;
Never will I forsake you."

Heb. 13:5 NIV

AUGUST 12

One joy scatters a hundred griefs.

Chinese Proverb

Cheerfulness is the atmosphere in which
all things thrive.

Jean Paul Richter

A cheerful look brings joy to the heart,
and good news gives health to the bones.

Prov. 15:30 NIV

MAY 22

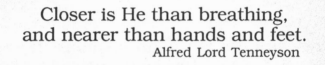

Closer is He than breathing,
and nearer than hands and feet.
Alfred Lord Tennyson

...in thy presence is fullness of joy; at thy
right hand there are pleasures for
evermore.   Ps. 16:11 KJV

AUGUST 11

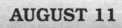

Lost— somewhere between sunrise and sunset, two golden hours, each set with sixty diamond minutes;
no reward is offered for they are gone **forever.**

Smiles

Teach us to number our days and recognize how few they are; help us to spend them as we should.

Ps. 90:12 TLB

MAY 23

We are shaped and fashioned by what we love.
Goethe

..."Love the Lord your God with all your heart and with all your soul and with all your mind." This is the first and greatest commandment.
Matt. 22:37 & 38 NIV

AUGUST 10

The great thing in the world is not so much where we stand, as in what directions we are moving..

Holmes

...open their eyes and turn them from darkness to light, and from the power of Satan to God, so that they may receive forgiveness of sins and a place among those who are sanctified by faith in me.

Acts 26:17 & 18 NIV

MAY 24

Your ship is equal to the load of today; but when you are carrying yesterday's worry and tomorrow's anxiety, you must lighten your load or you will sink.

Forgive me, Lord, for picking up burdens that I don't need to carry and for being anxious when I forget that You are in control. Thank You that I can lay this load at Your feet and with Your help I will not sink. Amen.

AUGUST 9

Where there is peace, God is.

Herbert

When a man's ways are pleasing to the Lord, he makes even his enemies live at peace with him.

Prov. 16:7 NIV

MAY 25

Bad things **do** happen to good people—
our response to it is what is important.

Know therefore that the Lord your God is
God; he is the faithful God, keeping his
covenant of love to a thousand
generations of those who love him and
keep his commands.   Deut. 7:9 NIV

AUGUST 8

"What are you doing?" a man asked of three laborers beside a building under construction.

The first man replied, "Puttin' in time until a better job comes along."

The second smiled. "Stone-cutting."

The third man waited a moment and then said simply, "I'm building a cathedral!"

Father, help me remember that each day I'm not just walking through life, but preparing for eternity. Amen.

MAY 26

A friend is the first person who comes in when the whole world has gone out.

A friend loves at all times...
Prov. 17:17 NIV

Thank you, Father, for my friend who loves me. Give me the patience and Your grace to be a loving friend in return. May we learn to keep You at the center of our relationship. Amen.

AUGUST 7

That silence is one of the great arts of conversation is allowed by Cicero himself, who says there is not only an art, but an eloquence in it.

More

Be still, and know that I am God;
I will be exalted among the nations,
I will be exalted in the earth.

Ps. 46:10 NIV

MAY 27

Duty makes us do things well,
but love makes us do them beautifully.

"And so I am giving a new commandment
to you now---love each other just as much
as I love you. Your strong love for each
other will prove to the world that you are
my disciples."

John 13:34 TLB

AUGUST 6

He who plants thorns must never expect
to gather roses.

...every good tree bears good fruit, but a bad
tree bears bad fruit. A good tree cannot bear
bad fruit, and a bad tree cannot bear good
fruit. Thus, by their fruit you will know
them.

Matt. 7:17,18 & 20 NIV

MAY 28

The same sun that melts the wax hardens the clay.

Lord, as the rays of Your sun shine down on me, help me choose to soften into love instead of hardening into bitterness. Amen.

AUGUST 5

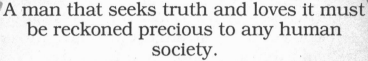

A man that seeks truth and loves it must be reckoned precious to any human society.

Frederick the Great

Jesus answered, "I am the way and the truth and the life. No one comes to the Father except through me..."

John 14:6 NIV

MAY 29

For the eyes of the Lord range throughout the earth to strengthen those whose
hearts are fully committed to Him.

II Chron. 16:9 NIV

*I need Your strengthening, Lord, and it is
so reassuring to know that even when I
forget to call to You, Your eyes are always
upon me. Amen.*

AUGUST 4

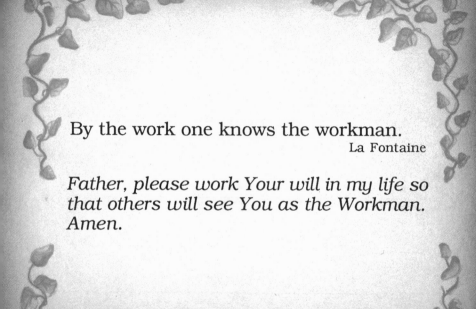

By the work one knows the workman.
La Fontaine

Father, please work Your will in my life so that others will see You as the Workman. Amen.

MAY 30

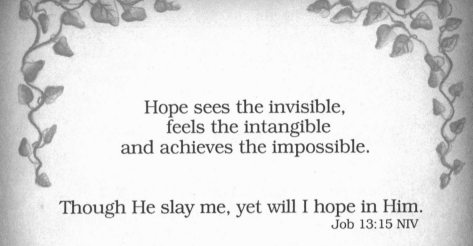

Hope sees the invisible,
feels the intangible
and achieves the impossible.

Though He slay me, yet will I hope in Him.
Job 13:15 NIV

AUGUST 3

All things proclaim the existence of God.
Napoleon

For since the creation of the world God's invisible qualities— his eternal power and divine nature— have been clearly seen...
Rom. 1:20 NIV

MAY 31

Do not say, "I'll do to him as he has done to me; I'll pay that man back for what he did."

Prov. 24:29 NIV

Lord, You know my heart. You under-stand how I have been hurt. Please give me the strength to place my hurt in Your hands and let go of the desire for revenge. Amen.

AUGUST 2

The really happy person is the one who can enjoy the scenery when he has to take a detour.

Commit to the Lord whatever you do, and your plans will succeed. The Lord works out everything for his own ends.

Prov. 16:3 & 4 NIV

JUNE 1

...I have summoned you by name;
   you are mine.
When you pass through the waters,
   I will be with you...
They will not sweep over you...
   because I love you.

Is. 43:1-4 NIV

*Lord, how my heart is filled with
thanksgiving as I remember this promise.
You are so faithful. Amen.*

AUGUST 1

If you want to pray better, you must pray more.

Mother Theresa

Pray continually; give thanks in all circumstances for this is God's will for you in Christ Jesus.

1 Thess. 5:17 & 18 NIV

JUNE 2

Enrich someone's life today with a warm word of praise. Both of you will be better for it.

Dear Father, open my eyes and help me see the good in others. I also ask Your help to overlook the faults in myself that others so graciously ignore in me. Amen.

JULY 31

When God gives any man wealth and possessions, and enables him to enjoy them, to accept his lot and be happy in his work---this is a gift of God.

Ecc. 5:19 NIV

Lord, thank You for all You have given me to enjoy. Make me aware of people in need with whom I can share from the abundance I have received. Amen.

JUNE 3

Children learn best from example; the trouble is, they don't know a good example from a bad one.

Train a child in the way he should go, and when he is old he will not turn from it.

Prov. 22:6 NIV

JULY 30

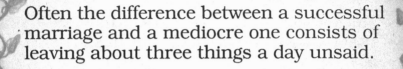

Often the difference between a successful marriage and a mediocre one consists of leaving about three things a day unsaid.

Father, please give me the desire and grace to say the things that I should say and to leave unsaid the things better left unsaid. Amen.

JUNE 4

Forgiveness is the fragrance that the violet sheds on the heel that has crushed it.

Be kind and compassionate to one another, forgiving each other, just as in Christ, God forgave you.

Eph. 4:32 NIV

JULY 29

Friendship is not a reward for our discrimination and good taste in finding one another.
It is the instrument by which God reveals to each of us the beauty of all the others.

C. S. Lewis

For my precious friend I am eternally grateful. The love and kindness of my friend encourages me to look for similar qualities in others I meet. Amen.

JUNE 5

The trouble with some self-made men is that they worship their creator.

A man's pride brings him low, but a man of lowly spirit gains honor.

Prov. 29:23 NIV

JULY 28

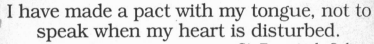

I have made a pact with my tongue, not to speak when my heart is disturbed.

St. Francis de Sales

..but he who holds his tongue is wise.

Prov. 10:19b NIV

JUNE 6

God often allows our hearts to be broken so that He can beautify our souls.

Before I was afflicted I went astray, but now I obey your word. It was good for me to be afflicted so that I might learn your decrees.

Ps. 119: 67 & 71 NIV

JULY 27

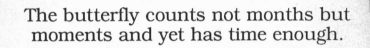

The butterfly counts not months but moments and yet has time enough.

Time—oh, Lord, how swiftly it seems to fly. Thank You for reminding me that there is time enough for what You have planned for my life. Amen.

JUNE 7

And I will give you a new heart— I will give you new and right desires— and put a new Spirit within you. I will take out your stony hearts of sin and give you new hearts of love. And I will put my Spirit within you so that you will obey my laws and do whatever I command.

Ez. 36: 26 & 27 TLB

JULY 26

It isn't so true that "prayer changes things" as that "prayer changes me and I change things."

Oswald Chambers

...Lord teach us to pray.
Luke 11:1 NIV

JUNE 8

There is no moment like the present. The man who will not execute his resolutions when they are fresh upon him can have no hope from them afterwards.

Edgeworth

Help me be aware, Lord, that today never returns. Give me a sense of stewardship of life that will make me want this day to count for You. Amen.

JULY 25

Choice, not chance, determines destiny.

Choose for yourselves this day whom you will serve,....as for me and my household, we will serve the Lord   Josh. 24:15 NIV

JUNE 9

Do it that very moment!
Don't put it off— don't wait.
There's no use in doing a kindness
If you do it a day too late!

Kingsley

Do not boast about tomorrow, for you do
not know what a day may bring forth.

Prov. 27:1 NIV

JULY 24

The great man is he that does not lose his child's heart.

Mencious

...whoever humbles himself like this child is the greatest in the kingdom of heaven.

Matt. 18:4 NIV

JUNE 10

True friends visit us in prosperity only when invited, but in adversity they come without invitation.   Theophrastus

Lord, You are my dearest Friend. Thank You that You are so close in my need that I don't even have to call. Help me learn to share Your friendship with others. Amen.

JULY 23

Nothing is impossible to a willing heart.
Heywood

Trouble and distress have come upon me, but your commands are my delight. Your statutes are forever right; give me understanding that I may live.
Ps. 119:143 & 144 NIV

JUNE 11

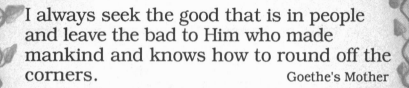

I always seek the good that is in people and leave the bad to Him who made mankind and knows how to round off the corners. Goethe's Mother

...as far as it depends on you, live at peace with everyone. Do not take revenge, my friends, but leave room for God's wrath... Rom. 12:18 & 19 NIV

JULY 22

Man is unjust, but God is just; and finally
justice triumphs.

Henry W. Longfellow

Do you want justice? Don't fawn on the
judge, but ask the Lord for it!

Prov. 29:26 TLB

JUNE 12

If you have knowledge, let others light their candles at it.　　　Fuller

Go into all the world and preach the good news to all creation. Whoever believes and is baptized will be saved, but whoever does not believe will be condemned.

Mark 16:15 & 16 NIV

JULY 21

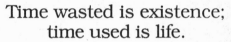

Time wasted is existence;
time used is life.

Young

...I have come that they may have life, and
have it to the full.

John 10:10 NIV

JUNE 13

God's goodness hath been great to thee;
Let never day nor night unhallowed pass,
But still remember what the Lord hath
done.   William Shakespeare

Praise the Lord.
Give thanks to the Lord, for he is good;
his love endures forever.   Ps. 106:1 NIV

JULY 20

The good you do is not lost though you forget it.

Do not repay evil with evil or insult with insult, but with blessing, because to this you were called so that you may inherit a blessing. I Peter 3:9 NIV

JUNE 14

The responsibility of tolerance lies with those who have the wider vision.

Eliot

Thank You, Father, that You did not create us all alike. Our differences add wonderful variety to our lives. Give us the grace to remember that You made us all different and You love us all alike. Amen.

JULY 19

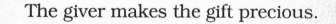

The giver makes the gift precious.

For God so loved the world that he gave his one and only Son, that whoever believes in him shall not perish but have eternal life.

John 3:16 NIV

JUNE 15

There are souls in this world who have the gift of finding joy everywhere and of leaving it behind them when they go.

But the fruit of the Spirit is love, joy, peace, patience, kindness, goodness, faithfulness, gentleness and self-control. Since we live by the Spirit, let us keep in step with the Spirit. Gal. 5:22 & 25 NIV

JULY 18

Be beautiful inside, in your hearts, with the lasting charm of a gentle and quiet spirit which is so precious to God.

I Peter 3:4 TLB

Dear Father, help me grow lovely inside as I grow older, remembering that growing older makes me closer to You. Amen.

JUNE 16

Our only greatness is that we aspire.

Ingelow

Teach me your way, O Lord;
Lead me in a straight path.

Ps. 27:11 NIV

JULY 17

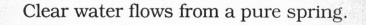

Clear water flows from a pure spring.

The Lord detests the thoughts of the wicked, but those of the pure are pleasing to him.

Prov. 15:26 NIV

JUNE 17

The blessedness of life depends more upon its interests than upon its comforts.   Macdonald

How can a young man keep his way pure? By living according to your word. I have hidden your word in my heart that I might not sin against you.

Ps. 119: 9 & 11 NIV

JULY 16

Build a little fence of trust around today,
Fill the space with loving deeds and
    therein stay;
Look not through the sheltering bars
    upon tomorrow,
God will help thee bear what comes of joy,
    or sorrow.

Butts

But make everyone rejoice who puts his
trust in you...because you are defending
them. Ps. 5:11 TLB

JUNE 18

I love little children, and it is not a slight thing when they, who are fresh from God, love us.

Charles Dickens

Help me remember, Father, that You created all life, that You knew me before I was born and knit me together in my mother's womb. May the love You planted in my heart continue to grow and spread to others. Amen.

JULY 15

He that can have patience can have what he will.

Franklin

He will give eternal life to those who patiently do the will of God...there will be glory and honor and peace from God for all who obey him...

Rom. 2:7-10 TLB

JUNE 19

All I have seen teaches me to trust the Creator for all I have not seen.

Ralph Waldo Emerson

Oh Lord, our Lord,
How majestic is your name in all the earth!

Ps. 8:9 NIV

Thank You, Lord, that over and over Your trust-worthiness is proven to me. Amen.

JULY 14

One is often sorry for saying a harsh word, but will never regret saying a kind one.

The mouth of the righteous is a fountain of life...wisdom is found on the lips of the discerning...   Prov. 10:11-13 NIV

JUNE 20

He is a wise man who does not grieve for
the things which he has not but rejoices
for those which he has.   Epictetus

But I trust in your unfailing love; my
heart rejoices in your salvation. I will sing
to the Lord, for he has been good to me.
                                        Ps. 13:5 & 6 NIV

JULY 13

Believe me,
 every man has his secret sorrows, which
the world knows not;
and oftimes we call a man cold, when he is
only sad.

Henry W. Longfellow

*I long to care about others as much as I
care about myself, Lord, and to give
others the benefit of the doubt just as I
hope others will do for me. Amen.*

JUNE 21

The secret of my success? It is simple. It is found in the Bible, "In all thy ways acknowledge Him and He shall direct thy paths."

George Washington Carver

Lord, it seems so simple, but Your Word is all I need. Amen.

JULY 12

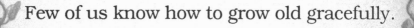

Few of us know how to grow old gracefully.

Teach us to number our days aright, that
we may gain a heart of wisdom.

Ps. 90:12 NIV

JUNE 22

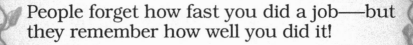

People forget how fast you did a job——but they remember how well you did it!

The plans of the diligent lead to profit as surely as haste leads to poverty.

Prov. 21:5 NIV

JULY 11

It is much easier to recognize error than to
  find truth;
for error lies on the surface and may be
  overcome;
 but truth lies in the depths...

Goethe

*I am often more willing to recognize error
in a friend, Lord, than to come alongside
and walk with that friend toward truth.
This day please help me make right
choices. Amen.*

JUNE 23

To get rid of an enemy, one must love him.

Leo Tolstoy

Do not gloat when your enemy falls; when he stumbles, do not let your heart rejoice.

Prov. 24:17 NIV

And Jesus said "...Love your enemies, do good to those who hate you..."

Matt. 6:27 NIV

JULY 10

It is never too late to give up our prejudices.

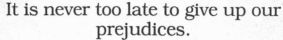

Thoreau

Father, You know the prejudices that I have hidden away in my heart, thinking that no one can see them. Help me be honest enough to bring them before You into Your light. Please fill that dark place with Your love. Amen.

JUNE 24

Let the words I speak today be soft and tender, for tomorrow I may have to eat them!

May the words of my mouth and the meditation of my heart be pleasing in your sight, O Lord, my Rock, and my Redeemer.   Ps. 19:14 NIV

JULY 9

The birds of the air nest by the waters;
they sing among the branches.
He waters the mountains from his upper
chambers; the earth is satisfied by the
fruit of his work.
He makes the grass to grow for the cattle,
and plants for man to cultivate --
bringing forth food from the earth...

Ps.104:12-14 NIV

...Praise the Lord, O my soul. Praise the
Lord.

Ps. 104:35 NIV

JUNE 25

Wisdom is a divine endowment and not a human acquisition.

If any of you lacks wisdom, he should ask God, who gives generously to all without finding fault, and it will be given to him.

Jam. 1:5 NIV

JULY 8

When you doubt the lovely silence of a
    quiet wooded place,
When you doubt the path of silver of some
    moonlit water space,
When you doubt the winds a'blowing,
Flash of lightning, glistening rain,
Sun or starlit heavens above you
On the land or bounding main,
When you doubt the sleep of loved ones
Deep beneath some precious sod,
Listen to a soft voice saying,
"Be still, and know that I am God."

Alicia Poole

JUNE 26

When a person is at his wits end it is not a cowardly thing to pray. It is the only way to get into touch with Reality.

Oswald Chambers

Lord, I often run here and there seeking help and comfort. Please give me the wisdom and courage to stop running and come to You in prayer. Amen.

JULY 7

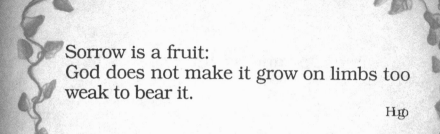

Sorrow is a fruit:
God does not make it grow on limbs too
weak to bear it.

Hugo

The Lord is close to the brokenhearted
and saves those who are crushed in
Spirit.

Ps. 34:18 NIV

JUNE 27

Submit to God and be at peace with him;
in this way prosperity will come to you.

Job 22:21 NIV

No one who has not tried it would believe
how many difficulties are cleared out of a
man's road by the simple act of trying to
follow Christ.

Alexander Maclaren

JULY 6

May every soul that touches mine—
Be it the slightest contact—
Get therefrom some good;
Some little grace; one kindly thought;
One aspiration yet unfelt;
One bit of courage
For the darkening sky;
One gleam of faith
To brave the thickening ills of life;
One glimpse of brighter skies
Beyond the gathering mists—
To make this life worth while...

George Eliot

JUNE 28

I don't mean to say I am perfect; I haven't learned all I should yet, but I keep working toward that day when I will finally be all that Christ saved me for and wants me to be.

Phil. 3:12 TLB

Father, thank You for the hope within me that every day I can be closer to what You would have me be. Please keep me faithful to the task. Amen.

JULY 5

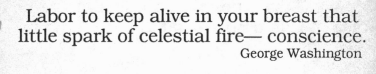

Labor to keep alive in your breast that little spark of celestial fire— conscience.

George Washington

So I strive always to keep my conscience clear before God and man.

Acts 24:16 NIV

JUNE 29

"I have lived, sir, a long time, and the longer I live, the more convincing proofs I see of this truth---that God governs in the affairs of men."

Benjamin Franklin

ThankYou,Father, for the wisdom of those who have gone before me. May I realize my responsibility to share my knowledge of You with others. Amen.

JULY 4

I don't think much of a man who is not wiser today than he was yesterday.

Abraham Lincoln

Let the wise listen and add to their learning, and let the discerning get guidance.

Prov. 1:5 NIV

JUNE 30

A house is not a home unless it provides food and warmth for the soul as well as for the body.

The Lord's curse is on the house of the wicked, but he blesses the home of the righteous.

Prov. 3:33 NIV

JULY 3

Praying is no easy matter. It demands a relationship in which you allow someone other than yourself to enter into the very center of your being, and to see there what you would rather leave in darkness, and to touch there what you would rather leave untouched.

Henri J.M. Nouwen

Dear Lord, please give me the courage to welcome Your light into those dark corners of my life. Amen.

JULY 1

I will lie down and sleep in peace, for you alone, O Lord, make me dwell in safety.

Ps. 4:8 NIV

How wonderful it is to have this reassurance from You, Father. Please help me remember these words when I lack Your peace and sleep is hard to find. Amen.

JULY 2